TIME WORKETH PATIENCE

MELODY KAY HEART

TIME WORKETH PATIENCE

This is a work of fiction. All of the characters, names, incidents, organizations, and dialogue in this novel are either the products of the author's imagination or are used fictitiously.

iUniverse books may be ordered through booksellers or by contacting:

iUniverse
1663 Liberty Drive
Bloomington, IN 47403
www.iuniverse.com
1-800-Authors (1-800-288-4677)

ISBN: 978-1-5320-4462-5 (sc)
ISBN: 978-1-5320-4463-2 (e)

Library of Congress Control Number: 2018908326

Print information available on the last page.

iUniverse rev. date: 09/06/2019

$\mathscr{A}$cknowledgements

My sincere appreciation goes out to my precious family and friends, who have been there for me. You have all endured all my life's plunders, loving and encouraging me through it all. I want to especially thank and dedicate my first novel, Time Worketh Patience, to two very special people. They are the ones who inspired me to write in the first place. Also, who helped encourage me to do my very best. The first person is my 5th-grade teacher, Doris. You always gave me a 100% or a Great Job, with smiley faces on my creative writing assignments you gave us in class. You are the first person who inspired me to write, getting my creative juices flowing, and I just want to say, "Thank you", from the bottom of my heart. You were one of my favorite teachers and I will never forget you. I give you 100% and happy faces always. Thank you for teaching me and being one of the best and greatest teachers I ever had.

The second person is one of my high school teachers, Leroy. What can I say? You were always there to show me your generous ways. You were always there for me to talk to about anything and everything. You were the one who got me my very first job, in working in the concession stand during football games. I really look up to you and admire you so very much. It was you who told me that you had all the confidence in the world in me, which made my day. I want to tell you, "Thank you, from the bottom of my heart, for encouraging me throughout the years. I will never forget you. And may God bless you both, above all you could ever imagine, now and throughout eternity.

But most of all, I want to thank our awesome heavenly Father God, giving Him all the Glory, Honor and Praise that He is so deserving of. Thank You, for every single solitary countless blessings that You so graciously bestow on me, on a daily basis, whether I'm deserving of them or not. Thank You, Jesus!

*P*rologue

It was the first day of freshman year in high school and Michelle was sitting in her third-hour English class in the front row by the door. Michelle was looking out the door when Mr. Fox walked by smiling and winked at her, making her smile too. At the time, she wasn't familiar who he was but thought he was very good looking. She was guessing he stood about 6"3. His hair was brown and was cut short, slender build with a golden dark tan. She could smell his nice smelling cologne when he walked by and was determined to find out just who he was. When the bell rang, Michelle filed out of the classroom, walking to her locker. As she walked by the principal's office, there he was again, standing with Mr. Alan who was the principal, laughing. Mr. Fox caught her looking at him and continued his conversation, watching her. Michelle bumped into the kid in front of her, dropping her purse on the floor. As she picked it up, she recognized who she bumped into, which was her best friend Dawn.

"Way to go Klutz! "I'm starving. Where are we eating lunch today?"

"Hey Dork, who is that guy back there talking to Mr. Alan?"

"I don't know?"

"Look! He's the tall, good looking one, standing by cute, baby face Mr. Alan."

"I don't know. Why? Go ask him." Michelle started laughing.

"No! I'm not going to go ask him."

After Michelle finally found out who he was, who was the 9th and 10th-grade counselor, Mr. Jesse L. Fox. Michelle kept running into him in the halls or he'd magically appear in one of her classes, showing up to talk to one of the students or the teacher. And every time, he spotted Michelle right off, smiling and winking at her. When it was time to pick up the schedules for sophomore year, she noticed that Mr. Fox was going to be teaching instead of counseling. She made the excuse that she wanted to be in Dawn's class when she went to his office to see if he could change it. It was miraculous that he actually changed her schedule for her and put her in Dawn's class, with him being the teacher, she thought. But what she didn't realize was that there was an actual mistake on her schedule.

Before Michelle knew it, she was sitting in her 10th-grade history class, on the first day of school, waiting for class to begin. She could hardly wait, having Mr. Fox as her teacher. It was the longest summer ever, she thought. He finally comes strutting in leisurely walking to his desk, opening his briefcase.

"Good morning class. My name is Mr. Fox. I look forward to meeting and getting to know each and every one of you. So, to start, I will call the roll. Just either raise your hand or say here or present when your name is called. When he called Michelle's name, he mispronounced it.

"My Shell Mertz."

"It's Michelle. here."

Michelle waited a whole year and the entire summer to finally be in his class, for him to mispronounce her name. OMG! Michelle thought.

"Oh, I beg your pardon. I'm sorry, Michelle."

"That's okay,"

Michelle told him, blushing.

Throughout the next three years of high school, Michelle had Mr. Fox as her history teacher, assistant basketball coach, bus driver, and counselor. When she found out that he drove the school bus down the street from her, she walked to the end of her street to catch it, instead of riding the one that stopped right in front of her house. Michelle really enjoyed being around him, having him as a teacher and mentor. Her senior year, she was his office aide. She could go to him with anything and he'd be there for her with encouraging words. After graduation, Michelle visited him at school, talking about all sorts of things, except for her feelings towards him. She really felt like he wanted her to call him by his first name now since she had graduated, but she just couldn't bring herself to for some reason. When he finally accepted her lunch invitation, after turning her down several times, she was so excited. Michelle wanted to tell him then, how she felt about him, but again, she was too shy and bashful. She knew he was married so she left well enough alone.

After she started working at the local grocery store, Mr. Fox came in from time to time, coming through her grocery line. Her legs always felt like rubber, when she saw him, being so delighted and still nervous. She didn't know why he made her feel like that but he did. Time passed and Michelle didn't see him come in the store anymore. She missed him but after she started dating a guy named Randy, steady for the next two years, she had moved on, although she always kept Mr. Fox close to her heart.

Chapter One

*D*awn, Michelle's best friend, came up the steps and walked into Michelle's house as Michelle was putting on her boots.

"Hey, Sis. Wow, this place is beautiful. I love the Victorian wrap-around porch!"

"Are you ready to go horseback riding, on Sara and Abraham? It is such a lovely April day to be riding."

"I'm ready if you are a Dork."

Michelle Mertz, 32, with long, blonde curly hair, 5"7, slender, medium build with a golden tan complexion and Hazel colored cat eyes. Dawn Carlyle, 32, with short straight blonde hair, 5"4, medium frame, fair colored skin, with blue eyes, have been best friends since high school. Fifteen years later, they still work together in the local grocery store and often refer to each other as sisters. Michelle was still single and never been married since she graduated high school. She worked two jobs, working as head cashier at Hometown Groceries, and recently landed a job being the caretaker of the Macafey's beautiful two-story Victorian style home, on a 12 acre Ranch near Gatlinburg, Tennessee. The house was white in color with a porch that wrapped around the entire house. It had seven bedrooms, seven in a half bath, with a grilling kitchen on the back porch with several porch swings in front and in the back.

The Macafey's were Missionaries who traveled to Honduras often, to minister God's Word and help build more churches. As they walked out to the huge red barn, they saw a blue Mustang drive by. Dawn smiled to herself, knowing who it was. Dawn was married with 2 children and was always fixing Michelle up on blind dates. Some Michelle knew about and some she didn't.

"So how long are the Macafey's going to be gone, Michelle?"

"I'm not sure exactly. They said they'd be keeping in touch from time to time, to just keep showing the house to good prospects. Sooner they sell this beautiful mansion, they can move to Honduras, they said."

As soon as they finished saddling Abraham and Sara, two, brown in color, blue-ribbon prize-winning Arabian horses; they trotted out of the barn.

"You know who I've been thinking about lately?" Michelle asked Dawn.

1

"Oh know, who?"

"Mr. Fox. I had a dream about him the other night."

"Mr. Fox, the teacher you had a major crush on in high school? I actually ran into him, literally, at The Garden Place last week. I was coming around the corner with my basket and "Boom!" He looked up and said, "Oops, are you okay?"

"And you are just now telling me this? What else did he say?"

"I recognized him right off, with his ugly eyebrows and big nose. I said, "I'm fine. Oh hey Mr. F., I mean Mr. Fox. I didn't mean to run into you. Sorry."

"That's okay; hum...Dawn is it? You used to be friends with Michelle Mertz."

"Yes, we still are from time to time."

Dawn laughed.

"How is she doing? Did she ever marry? She was such a sweet girl and always went that extra mile."

"Gee Mr. Fox, thanks for asking about me. No, she's still single, footloose and fancy-free."

"Yea, my wife has been gone a couple of years now and I have been alone ever since."

As Dawn was telling all this, Michelle was taking it all in as Dawn was talking and then just blurted out.

"I can't believe it! I just can't believe it!" Michelle said excitedly.

Michelle kicked her heels for Abraham to start running and he took off like the racehorse he was. She was laughing enthusiastically as Dawn tried to catch up to her.

"Michelle, wait! What can't you believe? Michelle!"

Dawn copied Michelle's lead and Sara took off, finally catching up to them, as the warm and sunny 85-degree breeze went whipping through Dawn's hair.

"Why did you do that? You don't still have feelings for him, do you? Oh Michelle, no. He's too old for you! Heck, he was old when we were in high school."

They heard a car racing down the country road and they both looked back to see. It was the blue Mustang again, that Dawn saw previously. Dawn recognized the blue Mustang, knowing it was Michael Viza, her husband's best friend, whom she was secretly fixing Michelle up with. Dawn told him that she was going to Michelle's to ride and that he ought to come out and look at the house for sale. He just moved to town and was staying at Dawn and Jakes house until he could buy a house, close to the hospital where he worked as a medical doctor.

"I wonder who that was! He needs to slow down! So, Mr. Fox, he still remembers me! And he's single now, may his wife rest in peace."

"Knowing you still have the hots for her husband, she'll probably come back and haunt your crazy ass! But he didn't say she passed away. He said that she left him. Look, the blue Mustang is coming back this way again. He must be lost. Look, I'll make a deal with you sis. If this guy in the mustang is single, have blue eyes and a hairy chest, ask him out to lunch. If anything different, I will take you out for lunch. Deal?" and then Dawn took off towards the fence.

"Dawn!"

Dr. Michael Viza drove slowly this time as he came up the road, stopping the car and looking at a piece of paper. Dawn on Sara ran up to the fence and stopped, as Michelle came alongside slowly. Michelle couldn't help but notice he did have a slightly hairy chest and he also had pretty blue eyes. His golden tan stood out amazingly with his 5 o' clock shadow around his jawline.

"May I help you? Are you looking for 1217 South Maple?" Michelle asked him.

"Why yes, yes I am, pretty lady. Do you know where that is?"

"First, don't be racing up and down this road as you have been! There are kids and animals that use this road too! You could hit or run them over."

"Yes, ma'am. I'm sorry. You are right. I shouldn't have done that."

"Michelle, ugh..."

Michelle gave Dawn a warning look, that Dawn has seen several times and was well aware of not to say anymore.

"If you promise me you will not let your lead foot race up and down this road again, I will tell you that the address you're looking for is the other direction, passed the two gigantic Maple trees and pond on the right."

"Thank you kindly ma'am and again, I'm sorry. I promise I will not drive like a maniac on this road ever again. I'll never let it happen again."

Michael drove off and turned around in the nearest driveway, which was three quarters of the way down from where he was. Michelle looked at Dawn again, after she watched Michael drive off.

"And how did you know, that he had blue eyes and a hairy chest? Dawn, if you are trying to get my mind off Mr. Fox, once again, I'm not going to be very happy with you."

"What. What's so wrong with that? Who knows? He could be the one Michelle." Michelle kicked her heels into Abraham again and he took off, leaving Dawn behind again.

Dawn took after her on Sara. As Michelle was getting closer to the red barn, Abraham came to an abrupt halt, rose up, throwing Michelle off; hitting her head on a rock and her left leg behind her. Once Dawn noticed Michelle on the ground, she made Sara run faster until she was by her side. Michael drove up just then, and got out, running over to Michelle. He ordered Dawn to get a wet cloth and meet him at his car. Michael then carefully picked Michelle up and gently sat her in on the passenger's side of his car. Dawn came back with the wet cloth he ordered and he wiped off the blood from her neck, and then placed it behind her head where she hit it.

"Is she going to be okay Michael? I sure hope so. Let's hope it's just a bump on the head."

Michelle opened her eyes, turned her head and moved her foot and groaned loudly, and then she passed out again.

"We need to hurry! I will follow you to the hospital."

They arrived at the hospital soon after they left the ranch. Michael called ahead and had a gurney waiting for her, rushing her into the ER. Dawn was soon at her side.

"Michael! She's opening her eyes again! Michelle, sis, can you hear me? Are you okay?"

Michelle looked puzzled, looking around. She looked up into Michael's pretty blue eyes and down to his slightly opened white polo shirt, seeing his hairy chest. Michelle then looked at Dawn with a half grin.

"No deal. He's no Fox. Owe! I have a pounding headache and my foot hurts baa..."

Michelle turned to throw up all over the floor, then fell unconscious again.

"What was she talking about Dawn? Didn't you tell her I was coming out to meet her and look at the house?

"No, not exactly. But I believe she knew what she was saying. See, I told her that I ran into one of our teachers from high school, that she evidently still has a crush on, and she reacted like she did back then. So, when I told you to come check out the house she was trying to sell, and to meet Michelle, I was hoping y'all would hook up, to get her mind off this old teacher. And so I told her if you had blue eyes and a hairy chest that she had to ask you out to lunch. And if you didn't, I'd take her out to lunch."

"Dawn! That's dirty pool! What kind of a friend are you anyway? Go wait in the waiting room while we X-Ray her head and foot."

"Ok Doc. Take good care of her! I love her like she's my very own flesh and blood sister."

Michael W. Viza, MD, standing at 5"8, medium stocky build with a dark tan. Michael been practicing for twelve years, in Galveston Texas, but wanted to move back home, where his parents and friends were. When Dawn told him about Michelle and the ranch house she was trying to sell for the Macafey's, he thought he could kill two birds with one stone. Dawn thought they'd be a perfect match, but she thought that with everyone she fixed her up with, as long as it wasn't Mr. Fox. Michael came out of the room, taking off his rubber gloves and throwing them away.

"Well, what's her diagnosis doc?"

"She definitely has a concussion and cracked her ankle bone. She will have a goose egg on the back of her head for a while and will have a mild case of amnesia. I'm going to keep her overnight for observation and see if her swelling goes down on her ankle before I cast it. I believe she will be okay. She just needs plenty of rest."

"Did she need stitches in her head?"

"Yes, I put seven stitches in, which isn't bad at all as hard as she hit the rock. She will be really stiff and sore, with some bruising, I'm sure. I cleaned her up pretty good and wrapped an Ace bandage around her head and ankle."

"How long will her Amnesia last?"

"It shouldn't last too long, probably just overnight. We don't know if she will remember what happened to her or where she is when she wakes up again. I gave her something for her pain and swelling, so she may sleep through the night. If not, I will have the nurse give her something stronger."

"Okay, thank you Michael. Maybe you can see the house when she is feeling better. I need to call Jake and tell him what happened. So are you going home tonight or stay here?"

"I'm going to visit my parents, and then I'll be going to the house. Why? Do you need anything?"

"Jake is working till 8 p.m. Will you please pick my kids up at my parents? I'll let them know you are coming by, please? I'm going to stay with Michelle until she wakes up again."

Michael agreed to pick up her kids and left. Dawn walked back in the room where Michelle was and shortly after, they wheeled her upstairs, to a regular hospital room. A few hours went by as Michelle slept. Dawn could hardly wait till Michelle woke up to see if she had Amnesia or not. The nurse came in to check her vitals. Michelle opened her eyes and looked around.

"Well looky here. Did you decide to be amongst the living?" Dawn asked Michelle.

"Where am I? Am I in the hospital?"

The nurse answered her.

"Yes honey, you're in the hospital. You were thrown off a horse."

"Yes, she's right Michelle. Abraham got spooked by a black snake and raised up, throwing you off. You hit your head pretty bad and have seven stitches. You also cracked your ankle."

"Everything is so fuzzy and I have a massive headache."

"Well your vitals are good, except your blood pressure is elevated a bit. But that is normal with your head trauma." The nurse said and exited the room.

"Michelle, what is the last thing you remember?"

"I remember us riding along and talking about...I'm so dizzy..."

Michelle leaned over the side of the bed then and she got sick. Dawn walked out of the room and went to get a nurse. When Dawn and the nurse walked back in, Michelle was still leaning over, getting sick.

Dawn went into the restroom to get a wet cloth and started wiping her forehead.

"Ms. Mertz, I'm going to give you something for your nausea and dizziness in your IV and it should work pretty quickly. Dr. Viza left orders to give you another pain reliever and a sleeping pill, to help you sleep all through the night. Is there anything else I can get you? My name is Barbie Castle, the head nurse."

"You might get someone to clean this up please." Dawn asked, pointing to the floor.

"Yes, ma'am, I intend to do that first thing."

"Michelle, sis, you should eat a bite or two of something."

"Yea, ugh...nothing sounds good. And I need to go to the restroom too."

"If you wait a minute, I will go get housekeeping to clean this up, go order a light dinner for you and then go get a wheelchair and help you to the restroom," Barbie said.

"Thank you, Barbie."

"Okay then, I will be back shortly." And she exited the room. When the nurse left the room, Michelle overheard her say hi to her grandpa and told him she'd be finished in a few minutes. Dawn remembered seeing a bedpan in the bathroom and chuckled to herself. She'd get the bedpan and show it to Michelle.

"Dawn, I am NOT using THAT!"

Dawn laughed out loud.

"I was just seeing if you had your wits about you, and you do." Dawn chuckled again.

"Well, wits or not, that wasn't funny."

Housekeeping came in and started mopping the floor as the nurse returned.

"Okay Ms. Mertz, I ordered you a light dinner plate, with chicken noodle soup and crackers. For dessert, I ordered you some strawberry sherbet, which I thought might feel good to your throat."

"That sounds good Michelle. You really ought to eat something since you hadn't eaten all day."

"You should be feeling some relief here pretty soon, especially after you eat some, with the meds we are giving you, and then you will probably be dozing off."

Barbie told Michelle, as she was administering the medicine in her IV.

"Is everything ok with her...Barbie?" as Dawn read her name badge, not remembering her name.

"Oh yea, she should be feeling better in the morning. This is normal, for what she has been through. A blow to her head like that causes a concussion, which causes all the symptoms she's having. Her blood pressure was a little high, not bad though, and running a slight fever. But all in all, she's doing pretty well."

"Ok, thank you, Barbie. You have been very helpful. Are you the head nurse up here? "Yes. In fact, they just gave me the position last year."

"Well, keep up the good work! I better go now, Michelle. I will see you in the morning."

"Yea, my grandpa came up here to take me to lunch. My car is in the shop, having some detail work done. I get it back Monday, hopefully. In fact, I better go find him. He might be flirting with some of the other nurses and or patients."

Dawn laughed as Barbie exited as a nurse's aide came and brought her light meal to her.

"Sis, you really need to try and eat. It will help you feel better."

Dawn walked over and took the lid off the soup and sherbet, then gave her a bite of soup.

"Sis, you don't have to feed me. I can feed myself. You better get home to Jake and the kids. I'll be fine. Go home."

"Ok dork. I will see you in the morning. Now eat!"

And Dawn exited.

Chapter Two

*I*t was 7:17 a.m. when Michelle woke up the next morning. She sat up slowly, putting her legs down from the bed. She felt really good and attempted to stand up and go to the restroom, but when she put all her weight on her cracked ankle, she fell to the floor. The wrap that was on her ankle had come off during the night, so she forgot she hurt it until she stood up on it. When she tried to get up, a guy walked by her room, saw her trying to get up, and came in to help her.

"Are you alright honey?" the good looking stranger asked. Michelle hadn't realized yet that it was Mr. Fox.

"Where were you headed? Let me get my granddaughter. She's the head nurse."

Mr. Fox hadn't realized that it was Michelle yet until he came back in with Barbie and Dr. Viza, pushing a wheelchair.

"What are you doing on the floor young lady?" Dr. Viza asked. "Well, I was feeling pretty good until I got up and tried to go to the restroom." Dawn came walking in just then.

"Way to go klutz!"

"Michelle, are you okay? I didn't recognize you honey."

Mr. Fox reached out to Michelle and patted her shoulder, as she realized that it was Me, Fox. Michelle was in shock and couldn't say a word.

"From the looks of your ankle swelling up like a balloon, you may have finished breaking it. Let's get you down to X-ray ASAP."

Dr. Viza saw that it was swelling and Barbie put an ice pack on it she brought back with her. They helped her into the wheelchair carefully and then wheeled her down to X-ray with Dawn and Barbie's grandpa, Mr. Fox following.

"So, Mr. Fox, what are you doing here?" Dawn asked.

"Barbie is my granddaughter. I came to pick her up from work. She's having her car detailed. I heard someone moaning as I walked by Michelle's room. I saw her lying there so helpless, but I was shocked to see it was Michelle! What happened?"

"Well, you know how clumsy she was in school. Do you remember her falling upstairs and all? She hasn't changed much. We were riding horses yesterday and the horse she was on got spooked by a black snake and the horse bucked her off. She hit her head, got a concussion and cracked her ankle. Oh and has stitches in the back of her head."

"Oh, poor baby. Is she going to be okay?"

"Oh, I'm sure she'll live. She sure hasn't got over you."

"Oh really? What makes you say that?"

"Remember when I literally ran into you with my cart while back? I just told her I saw you, while we were riding horses yesterday. She was ecstatic!"

Mr. Fox was laughing with pure joy. "Is that right? Well, bless her heart. What did she say?"

"Oh, good grief! You sound just like her! What did he say? Tell me, Dawn."

He laughed that much more.

"Let's just say she still has the hots for you, okay, and drop the subject. It's making me nauseous."

They had reached Radiology, which was a few halls away from Michelle's room. They waited outside in the hall while Dr. Viza and Barbie examined and X rayed Michelle. It seemed like an eternity waiting on them to finish with her, but they finally came wheeling her out with a cast on her ankle. When Michelle looked up at the tall stranger, she was taken back. Her memory suddenly came flooding back to her.

"Mr. Fox! What are you doing here!? Are you okay?"

He started laughing.

"I should be asking you that question, but Dawn was so gracious enough to fill me in. I'm just fine babe. How are you feeling now?"

"Well, it looks like you finished breaking it. Way to go klutz." Dawn popped off. Michelle started laughing and pointing and shaking her finger at Dawn.

"Ugh, I have a bone to pick with you sister."

"Yes, she broke it in the same three areas that were cracked alright. After the swelling went down some, I went ahead and cast it, as you can tell. I gave her a shot for the pain and swelling. She will need to keep it on for six weeks and of course off her foot propped up preferably. Michelle, I want to see you back in six weeks. You're free to go home. If you have any problems, be sure and let us know. Here is your prescriptions for the pain and swelling. And here is the doctor's note for work. Stay off that ankle and get plenty of rest."

"Thank you Dr. Viza."

Dr. Viza and Barbie exited the area.

"Grandpa, I will be ready in a few minutes. Dr. Viza wants to speak with me." Barbie said.

"Ok sweetheart." He looked back at Michelle.

"So you broke your ankle huh? I'm so sorry, my poor baby."

"You didn't do it, Mr. Fox."

"Michelle, please call me Jesse. It's okay. We are not in school anymore." Dawn cleared her throat as if to break the daze that Michelle and Jesse were in.

"Well Michelle, do you want me or ugh...Jesse here, to take you home?" Michelle started laughing with embarrassment, looking at Jesse and then Dawn.

"Dawn! You can't just impose on him like that. He may have other plans. Besides, I want to talk to you. Remember the bone I need to pick with you.....ugh concerning having lunch...?"

"I'm sorry Michelle, but as a matter of fact, I do have some important matters I need to tend with after I take Barbie home. You take care now. Obey the doctor's orders and I'll be seeing ya."

"Okay. It was nice seeing you again. You take care as well."

Jesse patted Michelle on the shoulder and gave her a gentle squeeze before he exited the area, walking down the hall to where Barbie was. Michelle watched him all the way down the hall. Michelle always enjoyed watching him walk, strolling sexy like. Dawn snapped her fingers in front of Michelle's face.

"Oh, earth to Michelle. Come in Michelle."

"What! I'm here. Yes, I'm ready to go home."

"Okay hateful! I ought to make you walk home."

Dawn started pushing Michelle back to her room to change into the clothes Dawn brought for Michelle. And then they both left after Dawn went to bring the car up to the door as a nurse aide helped Michelle into the car. Michelle was looking out the window, her thoughts were on Jesse. How she fantasized about him for years and seeing him again, it flooded her mind with so many memories.

"Michelle, what did you think of Michael? Dr. Viza? He is pretty cute, huh?"

"What did you say, sis, I'm sorry."

"You were zoning clear out there. What were you thinking about, or do I already know?" Michelle started laughing again.

"I can't believe I saw Mr. Fox, I mean Jesse. Oh, that sounds strange calling him by his first name. He still looks hot in his blue jeans!"

"Please, Michelle. Don't get messed up with him again. Leave the old poot alone. Find someone closer to our age, like Dr. Michael Viza. He's not married and I think he took a liking to you."

"Oh yes, that reminds me. Just how do you know this Dr. Michael Viza anyway? I know you know him Dawn and trying to fix me up with him. How else would you know he had blue eyes and a hairy chest? Huh? Tell me now Dawn."

"Okay, okay! Yes, I know him. He's Jakes best friend. They are like brothers like you and I are sisters. Michelle! He's a doctor for God's sake. He has mucho money and he did come to look at the house. He moved back from Texas to be close to his parents and Jake. He is staying with us until he finds a place of his own."

"Well isn't that special. As for him liking me, he doesn't seem interested in me in the least. Especially the way he was flirting with Barbie."

"Oh really?"

"Yes, oh really."

"Well, we are here, home sweet homegirl. Homegirl! That's funny!"

"Dawn, you are such a nut!"

"Well sis, it takes one to know one. I learned from you."

They drove up to the Victorian ranch home. Dawn parked and helped Michelle out of the car, giving her the crutches that they gave her at the hospital. Dawn got her up the stairs and into the house, sitting her on the sofa. Michelle got situated on the sofa and turned on the television, while Dawn fixed them a glass of sweet tea. Michelle flipped through the channels and saw her favorite TV preacher was on.

"Oh Dawn, Dr. Charles is on. This is the one who I wanted you to listen to."

"What denomination is he?"

"Baptist, but it doesn't matter really, what denomination, as long as they preach the love of God and that Jesus died for all sins, and whoever believes in Him should not perish, but have everlasting life and have it more abundantly. And that no man can come to the Father but by Him. Jesus is God's Son."

Dawn came and sat down, handed Michelle her glass of tea and continued watching the program.

"How are you doing sis? Is the medicine Michael gave you kicking in yet?"

"Yea, I believe so. I'm feeling kinda drowsy."

"Do you want me to get you anything else, a pillow, a blanket?"

"Yes, will you get my pillow off the bed and the blanket at the foot of the bed, please? I'm staying in the guest's bedroom, down the hall, across from the office."

"You got it, sis. Be right back."

Chapter Three

*D*awn headed down the hall, but couldn't resist taking a full tour of the beautiful mansion. When Dawn returned a few minutes later, Michelle was fast asleep. Dawn covered her up and propped Michelle foot upon her pillow. Then she wrote her a note, leaving it on the end table by her tea glass before she left. It was 3:00 p.m. before Michelle woke up. She got up with her crutches and found the note Dawn left on the table. It read:

> *Home Girl,*
>
> *Didn't want to wake you when I left. Sorry it took me so long to bring you your pillow and blanket. I uh, got lost, on purpose, taking a tour of the mansion. So beautiful! I enjoyed watching Dr. Charles. You are right. He's pretty good. I will call you after I feed my family. Take it easy and stay off your foot as much as you can. Talk to you soon.*
>
> *Your sis always,*
> *Dawn*

Michelle laughed at her note, laying it back on the table. "She's such a goober." Michelle got up and used her crutches to go to the restroom, then into the kitchen to fix her a glass of milk and peanut butter and jelly sandwich. She was wondering how she was going to take care of this place now that she's laid up and needs to stay off her ankle.

Michelle begins to pray:

> *"Dear Father God, in Jesus name, please help me to heal quickly so I can continue to do my job around here. But in the meantime, please send laborers, ugh cheap ones preferably, to help me. Thank You in advance. And bless this food for the nourishment of my body. I love you. Amen."*

Michelle often prayed out loud because that is the way she was taught.

"God likes to hear your voice, her aunt always told her. After Michelle ate her sandwich and drank her milk, she went into the office and started working on her novel. Time passes quickly and before Michelle knew it, it was 7:37 p.m. Michelle closed her laptop and got up, going to her bedroom and put on her nightshirt. She crawled in bed, reaching for her Bible when the phone rang.

"Hello?"

"Hey, homegirl. How are you feeling?"

"I'm kinda tired. I had been working on my novel all afternoon."

"That's good. You about finished with it?"

"Yea. I just crawled into bed and was going to read my Bible until I felt sleepy enough to go to sleep."

"Hey, I liked that Dr. Charles guy. He really said some stuff I agreed with."

"See, I told you'd like him. I got your note. So did you enjoy your tour of the house, did you?"

"Oh, yea. I loved it! I can't believe no one has bought it yet."

"There have been a few that have looked at it, I think out of curiosity but no takers yet."

"Hey, I talked to Jake and he agreed that he and I will help you take care of things while your ankle heals. Me and the kids will come by in the morning and clean house and feed the horses for you. The kids said they would clean the barn. And Jake said he'd come by around noon and start mowing and then clean the pool."

"Awe sis, really? Thank you. Thank You, Jesus! Praise God!! I prayed today that God sends me help and for a speedy recovery. God is so good Dawn. Thank you so much and please thank Jake too and the kids for me."

"Girl stop it. What are friends for? You have done so much for me, it's time I start repaying you in return. Just don't worry about anything but getting better. We will see you in the morning at around 10ish. Is that okay?"

"Yes, that will be just fine. Thank you again, sis. I truly appreciate it."

They ended their call and Michelle read a couple of chapters out of Hebrews and fell asleep.

It was 9:12 a.m. when Michelle woke up. She laid there for a little bit before she got up and went about her morning ritual. After she finished getting dressed, she went to unlock the front door and opened it. As Dawn said, she arrived around 10, with a box of donuts and two chocolate milks in her hand. Her two kids, little Jacob, who was seven, blonde hair and fair skinned like his mom. Danielle, who just turned three, long blonde curly hair and blue eyes came rushing up the porch steps and in the house, bumping Dawn, dropping and spilling their chocolate milk on the wood floor, not missing a beat running to Michelle.

"Hi, Aunt Michelle! Can I draw on your cast? Mom said you broke it."

"Sure Jakey."

"Me too Aunt Shell?"

"Yes, you too dumplin. Can I have a hug from you two first?"

They both hugged Michelle and with a marker already in their hands, they brought from their home, started drawing on her cast.

"No me first, me first!" Danielle started crying' trying to push Jacob out of the way.

"No, me! I'm the oldest. Get back, baby!"

"I'm not a baby!" Dawn scolded both of them.

"Kids! Both of you stop now! Get over here! No one is drawing on Aunt Michelle's cast until each of you clean up this chocolate milk off the floor!" The kids were still fighting, as Dawn started counting.

"One! Two! If I get to three, you both are getting spanked." They both got up and went over by their mom.

"That's what I thought! Here, use these napkins to wipe it up with and you better tell Aunt Michelle sorry for spilling milk on her floor and for acting up."

"But I'm not the one who bumped you, it was Danielle."

"Jacob Ryan!"

Dawn handed them some napkins, giving Jacob a warning look and they started wiping up the milk. Jacob made a face at Danielle and she stuck her tongue out at him as Dawn was watching them both.

"Guys, what did I say in the car on the way over here?"

"That if we weren't good, that our butts would get spanked and not be able to ride the horses," Jacob said hesitantly.

"Okay then. Very good. Did you get all the milk up?"

"Yes. I'm sorry mommy and Aunt Michelle." Danielle said.

"Jacob?"

"I'm sorry too."

"Ok, thank you, you two. Now Danielle, slowly go give Aunt Michelle her bottle of chocolate milk and Jacob, carry this box of donuts over and give it to her."

The kids did as they were told.

"Now, you may one at a time, draw on her cast."

"Why don't you get on this side Jacob and, Danielle get on my side? There you go. Now you both can draw at the same time."

"I'm going to draw a horsey!" Jacob said enthusiastically.

"Well, I am going to draw a heart and flowers," Danielle repeated enthusiasm.

Dawn was looking at Michelle, shaking her head in dismay.

"Oh, they are good kids Dawn. Let them be."

"At times, they try my patience."

"So, what is Dr. Michael Viza up to today?"

"Not really sure. He's probably looking for a place to live. Why are you asking about him? I thought you weren't interested since Mr. Fox is back in the picture."

"I was just curious. He is pretty cute. And those blue eyes, very attractive." Dawn started laughing.

"Yes, he is that for sure. Well, I better get started cleaning. Where shall I start sis?"

"My basket is full of clothes and towels. You should know where the laundry room is since you toured the place yesterday." Michelle started laughing.

"Looky Aunt Michelle! You like my horsey?"

"Awe Jakey, he looks really good buddy! Is that Abraham?"

"Yep, sure is!"

"Look at mine Aunt Shell! Do you like mine too?"

"Very pretty Danielle! I love them both! Now you need to write your names by your pictures so people will know who drew them."

"Ok." They both said in unison.

"Danielle, I will help you write your name if you need me to."

"That's really nice of you Jacob," Dawn told him, as he took the marker Danielle was giving him.

"What do you tell him, Danielle?"

"Thank you, Bub."

"When daddy gets here kids, you can start cleaning the barn. But until then, you can help mommy clean Aunt Michelle's house and help with the laundry."

"Ok mommy. What is Aunt Michelle going to do?"

"Uncle Michael told her to stay off her foot so it can heal."

As Dawn headed for the laundry room to start washing, Jacob and Danielle followed after her. Michelle picked up a magazine from the table and started looking through it.

Chapter Four

A few days later, Michelle and her mom went to go eat at a Chinese buffet in town. As they were seated, Michelle couldn't believe her eyes, seeing who was sitting across the restaurant. She kept her eyes on him, as he was reading a newspaper. The waitress came and took their drink orders and brought them silverware.

"Mom, see that gentleman sitting over there reading the paper?"

"Yea, who is he? Do you know him?"

"Yea, he was one of my teachers in high school."

"Oh, he was? He doesn't look much older than you. How old is he? Is he married?"

"No, he's widowed, or something."

"Then go for it girl! You're not in school anymore dear."

"You really want me to get married, don't you?"

"No honey, I'm not. But I do know you want to someday. I just want you to be happy Michelle."

"I am happy mom. I'm blessed in fact. Do you remember the teacher I had a wild and crazy crush on?"

"I remember you had a crush on a teacher, but..."

Michelle's mom, Edith Mertz was trying to recall the teacher's name. "Mr. Fox!" she said rather loudly, surprised she recalled his name. "Shhh, mom! Yes, him. Oh great, he heard you, along with everyone else in the place! How embarrassing!"

Jesse looked up from his newspaper then and smiled, seeing Michelle shrinking down in her chair from embarrassment. Jesse laughed but kept reading his paper and Michelle was very thankful he didn't come over.

"You liked him a lot, didn't you? Is that him? You should go over and talk to him."

"Ugh mom, in case you forgot, I have this cast on."

"He's the one who let you take your final exam a few days later because you had chicken pox. You were so mad at your niece and nephews for giving you chicken pox. You missed I think two weeks, didn't you? And you missed the Spring Fling that one day too. I remember you begged me to let you go to school that day."

16

"Yes, I remember like it was yesterday. I had Dawn take pictures for me."

Her mom continued to ask her questions about Jesse, making Michelle laugh out loud, and then Edith went to go get their plates. Jesse watched, looking up from his paper, hearing her all too familiar laugh. Edith arrived back at their table, placing Michelle's food in front of her.

"Thanks, mom. It looks rather delicious." "I got all your favorites, I think. So, how many kids does he have? How old are they?"

"Mom!" Michelle quietly scolded her and looked across the way to see if Jesse was still seated. He was watching her, smiling. Michelle smiled back and took a bite of her Sesame Chicken.

"He has two grown kids, not sure how old they are."

"How old did you say he was?"

"Fifty-something, I think, but I'm not sure."

Michelle took another bite of her food, looking again towards Jesse, which never took his eyes off her. He took a drink of his white wine slowly and winked at Michelle. Edith kept interrogating her until she answered her every question about him. All through lunch, Jesse looked up from his paper from time to time to admire Michelle.

Jesse finished his white wine and walked up to their table. "Hi, Michelle. We better stop meeting like this or people may start talking. How are you Love?"

"Let them talk. Hi, I am her mother, Edith Mertz." Edith reached her hand over to shake his hand.

"Mom! You are so embarrassing!"

"What. I was just introducing myself."

Jesse started laughing, patting Michelle on her bare shoulder. after shaking hands with Jesse.

"You better be nice to your mom. You have her beautiful green eyes." He smiled at her mom winking at her.

"Why thank you, Jesse is it?"

"Yes, ma'am."

"Michelle has told me so much about you, I feel like you are part of the family." Jesse laughed his hearty laugh Michelle loved hearing.

"Please forgive my mother Jesse."

"It is a great pleasure meeting you Edith. You have a very lovely daughter."

"The pleasure is all mine. Michelle has talked highly of you for years. I remember her coming home sometimes, beaming from ear to ear, because of something you said or done. Other times, she'd come home with a frown bigger than Texas, because you were either not at school or you were talking to..."

"Mom! Didn't you have to go to the restroom?"

Jesse was still laughing at the two of them tickling his fancy as her mom excused herself from the table.

"Please excuse me. I have to rinse my false teeth out because a Sesame seed got stuck underneath and it feels like gravel."

"Oh my Gosh, mom!"

Jesse was doubled over laughing at this point. Michelle was beaten red with embarrassment, laughing too.

"My mother. I can't believe her at times."

"Enjoy every minute you have with her Michelle. She's a delightful lady and so is her daughter."

Jesse was looking at Michelle, winked and smiled, caressing her shoulder. Michelle enjoyed his gentle warm touch and smiled.

"So, how are you feeling babe?"

"Pretty good. As you can tell, I am still on crutches, but I believe it is healing well."

"Well, that's good to hear. When were you going back to the doctor?"

Edith came back and sat down.

"He said in six weeks, but I think I will call and get an appointment sooner than that."

Jesse looked at his watch.

"Well, I better let you two finish your lunch. Edith, it was my pleasure meeting you and Michelle has spoken highly of you too, in school. You have a very beautiful daughter."

"Oh, I bet she did. Thank you, Jesse. I was going to tell you that your name suits you well because you are a fox."

"Mom! For the love of God, stop embarrassing me!"

Jesse laughed again; his hearty laugh.

"Well, I don't know about that, but I think a lot of Michelle too. She's a special lady who always went that extra mile. She was such a good student and helped me out a lot. I don't know what I'd have done without her."

Michelle looked up at him and smiled that pretty smile he loved so much when he winked at her. Jesse reached across the table to shake Edith's hand and took the meal ticket off the table nonchalantly.

"Edith, it was a pleasure. Michelle, be good to your mom and take care. I'll be seeing ya."

Jesse left, disappearing behind the wall where the cashier was and paid for their meals along with his. He waved to them as he walked out the door to his car.

"Michelle, I like him. He's really nice, sexy and very charming."

"I can't believe you thoroughly embarrassed the crap outta me like that!"

"Oh Michelle, he was getting a kick out of it. I was simply complimenting him how attractive he was."

"I know, but did you have to do it in front of me, in public!?"

Edith started looking around for the meal ticket.

"Michelle, did you take the meal ticket?"

"No, I thought you took it when you went to the restroom."

"No, I didn't." They both looked on the floor and all around when the waitress came to their table, carrying a chilled bottle of white wine.

"The fine-looking gentleman that recently left wanted me to give you this and tell you that lunch was on him. He paid for your meals. He's very generous and so kind."

"Thank you Madyson." as Michelle looked at her name badge.

Madyson bowed to them and went back behind the wall.

"Oh what a sweetheart he is. Michelle, if you don't nab him, I will!"

Michelle started laughing.

"Ugh, I don't think dad would like that very much mom."

"Oh, he wouldn't mind." Michelle laughed again as she got up and Edith going up to Madyson again to offer her a tip.

"No, no. He took care of that too. Mr. Fox comes here often. He is very generous. Also, he is very good-looking. In fact, he offered to help pay for me to buy my own shop so I could run my own Chinese café. I'm sorry I'm rambling. Thank you, ladies. Come back soon."

"That was extremely nice of Jesse to pay for our meals and buy us this bottle of wine. I bet it was the kind he was drinking at his table."

Edith's car was making a strange sound when she started it up, so she got out and looked underneath the hood but couldn't find anything.

Edith and Michelle left and arrived back at the Victorian ranch. As Edith drove off, Michelle heard her cell phone ring. She dug it out of her purse and sat down on the porch swing.

"Hello?"

"Hello. Is this Michelle Mertz?"

"Yes, it is. May I help you?"

"I was calling about the house you have for sale."

Michelle felt like she had heard the voice before, but couldn't place it.

"May I ask who's calling? Your voice sounds familiar." There was a brief pause, and then she heard Jesse laughing.

"Mr. Fox! Is that you?" He was laughing from trying to disguise his voice and her response.

"Yes, yes it's me. But please start calling me by Jesse, Michelle."

"Okay, but Jesse Michelle sounds awfully funny."

"You silly goose. So did you enjoy lunch as much as I did?"

"Yes, very much so. Jesse, thank you. You didn't have to do that. And thank you for the nice bottle of wine too."

"I enjoyed meeting your mom. She's a card."

"Yea, she's a joker alright."

"She seems to enjoy tormenting you."

"Ugh yea, a little too much I'm afraid. Torturing me is more like it."

"I was looking through the paper, as you know, and saw a house for sale, on a Country Road, with this phone number. Is this your house?"

"Yea, right. No, about three months ago, I saw this ad in the paper that struck my fancy. These people are Missionaries and were looking for someone to stay in their house and to take care of things around here while they were gone."

"You didn't put their house up for sale did you?"

"No, Jesse, listen. They needed someone to keep up their house for them and everything around here and try to sell it for them. They put the house up for sale. Not me, silly goose." she mocked him.

"They paid me $1000 a month, plus room and board. So I called them and they interviewed me. And wham, here I am. Cool, huh? So, are you interested in buying a house, Jess?"

"I might, you never know. I would definitely like to see it. It sounds really nice. But I don't think I would be able to afford a mansion like that. I don't have that kind of money Michelle."

"Sure you do."

"No, I don't either. Remember how I always talked about how teachers should be paid more money?"

"Yea, I remember. Maybe the Macafey's, the Missionaries, will come down on their price. They have lowered it, little by little since they put it up for sale."

"Really? Well maybe then. Where are they Missionaries at?"

"Honduras. They are helping to build more churches."

"Where do you go to church Michelle?"

"Where I've always gone, P.F.C., Pigeon Forge Christian church. You ought to come to visit sometime Jesse."

"Maybe I will. I will bring my granddaughter, Barbie."

"Then afterward, we can go have lunch?"

"Are you asking me out, Michelle?"

"Only if you will accept." He laughed.

"Well, we could probably do that. Go have Chinese food or something?"

"You bet! I could eat Chinese food every day. So...when is this going to take place, Jess?"

"Don't you think we ought to wait until you get your cast off first, and off the crutches?"

"I guess you're right. It would be better not hobbling along."

"Aren't I always right?" Jesse challenged her.

"No. No one is "always" right, except for Jesus. Hey, have you ever watched a tall, slim white-haired man preacher, by the name of Dr. Charles?"

"No, I don't recall that I have. What station does he come on and what time?"

"Sunday evenings, on the Christian channel at 9 p.m... That is your homework, Mr. Jesse L Fox. Let me know how you like him, okay?"

"Yes ma'am, I will find it and watch him and let you know. I better let you go so you can rest. Stay off your foot so it can heal quickly. The faster it heals, the sooner we can have lunch together. Who's been helping you around the house with the chores and stuff?"

"Some good looking farm hands I hired."

"Oh, I see. Are they getting the job done?" Michelle started laughing.

"You know I haven't hired anyone like that. Dawn and her family have been helping me and my twin nephews, Robert and James. And my niece, Angela. That reminds me, do you remember when I introduced her to you as my aunt, instead of my niece? I was so nervous around you."

Jesse started laughing.

"Yes, I remember that. Why were you nervous around me Michelle? Are you still nervous around me?"

Michelle paused before she answered him, and then tried to change the subject. "Michelle?"

"Yes and no. So were you going to offer to help if I didn't have any help around here?"

"Yes, if you still need help, I'm available. I was raised on a farm. I know how to be a farmhand."

"That's sweet of you Jess, thank you."

"Well, I better let you rest now. I will talk to you soon. Take care of yourself and be careful. By Love."

"Okay, thank you for calling and for the wine and buying lunch today Jess. I shall see you in church soon too, and don't forget to watch Dr. Charles."

"Okay babe, see ya."

Michelle had a big smile on her face when she hung up with Jesse. He had been all she's thought about off and on, through the years, but especially since Dawn told her she had run into him and that he asked about her and he was available. She went inside the house, going into the office to continue writing. She was anxiously waiting for her first novel to be published while she was writing on her second novel. Michelle loved writing. It helped her relax and escape from the real world, giving her something to look forward to with hopes of getting published and one day, turning her novels into movies as well. Before Michelle knew it, it was going on 9 p.m. She had been writing part of the afternoon and into the evening. She closed her laptop and hobbled to her bedroom across the hall to get ready for bed, then climbed in and fell asleep.

Chapter Five

*M*ichelle woke up to the sound of rain blowing against the window and thunder booming loudly. She got up and hobbled to the window to look out. The rain was standing out in the front yard in spots. She hobbled to the restroom, as her cell phone rang. Michelle hobbled back into the bedroom to get her phone and answered it.

"Good morning Dork. How's it going?"

"Good morning sis. Okay. I just got up. What are you up to?"

"Oh not much. Jake went to work and the kids and I are baking cookies."

"Sounds like fun. Yea, mom took me out to lunch yesterday and guess who we ran into?"

"Who?"

"Jesse."

"Oh great!"

"Stop! Just listen. He stopped by our table before he left and chatted with us a few minutes. Mom thoroughly embarrassed the crap outta me, several times in front of him! Good night, she just doesn't let up! He took our meal ticket and paid it for us and bought us a bottle of white wine."

"Wow, what was that for?"

"Not sure. Just being friendly I guess."

"Michelle, this fantasy you have about you and Mr. Fox is never going to work out so you might as well give it up."

"For your information, he called me yesterday after I got home. We had a very nice conversation."

"How did he get your number? Did you give it to him?"

"No, he saw the house for sale in the paper with my phone number."

"He must have remembered me telling him you were trying to sell a house for some missionaries or something."

"It was kinda funny because when he called, he was trying to disguise his voice for a little while, then he started laughing."

"Hmmm, that is interesting. It just sounds fishy to me. What is he up to? Just be careful Michelle."

"You are reading way too many mystery novels Dawn, and reading way too much in this. Goodbye sis."

Michelle hung up with Dawn, went to the kitchen to toast her raisin muffin and fix her some coffee with cream. As she was going back into the living room, her cell phone rang again.

"Hello?"

"Good morning Beautiful. Did you sleep well?"

"Good morning Jesse. Yes, I did, thank you. Did you?"

"Yes, finer than frog's hair."

She started laughing.

"Well, that's pretty fine."

There was a pause.

"Jess, are you still there?"

The phone went silent for a few seconds, and then Jesse came back on the line.

"I'm sorry Michelle. That was Sophia, ugh, my neighbor."

"Your neighbor? Is she alright?"

There was another brief pause, then she heard a woman laughing in the background.

"Michelle? Are you there? I'm sorry Love, but my cell phone is cutting in and out. I can barely hear you. Let me call you on my house phone."

"Don't bother.", and Michelle ended the call while he was still talking. Hearing a woman laughing in the background made her upset. She put her phone on silent and clicked on the television, switching it over to Godflix, to try and find a Christian movie to watch. She loved watching movies and loved going to the movies as well. As she was looking for a movie to watch, she noticed Jesse was trying to call her back, but she didn't want to talk to him. His neighbor was obviously more important so why did he even call her? Michelle found a cute looking movie and proceeded to watch it, as her phone was lighting up again but she continued to ignore it.

Michelle watched the entire 2 1/2 hour movie, but she couldn't help think about what Dawn told her how fishy Jesse seemed to her, and that women's laugh she heard in the background while she was talking to Jesse on the phone. Her thoughts were interrupted when she looked down at her phone to see if he had tried to call anymore. 3 missed calls from the same number, and her phone lit up again. It was her mom.

"Hi, mom. How's it going?"

"Doing well honey. How are you doing? How is your ankle?"

"Oh, it's still there."

"Well, I hope so dear. Hey just wanting to know if you need anything? Dad and I will be out and about today, running around."

"No mom, I can't think of anything. Thank you though. Going to run in the rain?"

"It's fixing to let up and forecasted to be in the lower 80's today with sunshine."

"Oh well, that's good then. Be careful. I'll talk to you later.", and Michelle ended the call.

Michelle got up from the sofa and went about doing little chores. When she hobbled back in the living room, she saw someone standing on the front porch, holding a vase full of pink and white roses, in front of his face so she couldn't tell who it was. She made it to the door and opened it.

"These are for you, Ms. Mertz. Please accept my apologies from earlier on the phone?"

"Jesse, there isn't any need for an apology, is there?"

Jesse came in, carrying the flowers and sat them in front of the sofa on the coffee table and turned to look at her as she was making her way to sit down.

"How did you know where I lived? The address wasn't in the paper."

Michelle sat down on the sofa and Jesse sat beside her.

"No, but when Dawn mentioned you selling a house out in the country by Kingridge Falls, I thought I'd take a chance and try and find you."

Michelle was looking at him suspiciously.

"Thank you for the pretty roses. So, why was your neighbor over and why was she laughing?"

"Michelle, it's nothing to worry your pretty little head about. Her electricity went out during the storm and she came over. She should have known mine was off too. She's nuts really. We have been neighbors for years."

"Is that right? Years?" she said hatefully.

"Somethings bothering you. What is it? And what did you mean when you said yes and no when I asked you if you were still nervous around me?"

Michelle was looking at him, as he was studying her, trying to determine why she had an attitude. Michelle spoke first.

"I want to know the truth, Jesse. No BS. First, why was your neighbor really over your house? Did she spend the night...?"

Jesse started laughing, being amused that Michelle was so concerned about his neighbor. So he added more fuel to the fire.

"Why, are you jealous?" Michelle looked away from him then and looked out the window. Jesse reached for her hand and she moved it away from him.

"Michelle, she didn't stay the night. She simply came over to bring me my newspaper because it landed in her yard."

"Why was she laughing?"

"Who knows? She's fruitier than a fruitcake. Michelle, look at me Babe, please." Without looking, she asked him again, how he knew how to get to the house.

"If you must know, I followed you and your mom yesterday."

Michelle looked at him in shock and disbelief.

"Why on earth did you do that? Are you stalking me now?"

"I saw your mom look underneath the car hood in the parking lot at the Chinese buffet yesterday, and I wanted to make sure you made it home ok."

Michelle started softening after he told her that and turned to look at him then.

"Heart and mind clear now?"

"Did you follow mom home too, to make sure she made it home okay as well?"

"Yes Love, I did."

"Okay, thank you."

"So, are we good now? You look awfully cute when you're mad at me."

Michelle smiled and chuckled, turning her head away with embarrassment.

"And you are adorable when you get embarrassed."

"Jesse, will you stop, please, and change the subject."

"Okay, so tell me the whole story how you hurt your ankle."

"I thought Dawn told you,"

Yes, but I want to hear it from you."

"Well, I invited Dawn to come over and ride with me, to exercise the horses, so when she came, that's what we did. She told me about running into you at the garden place and all."

"And all?"

"That you had asked about me and that your wife passed away a couple of years ago. You can imagine how it made me feel. Sorry about your loss by the way. As we raced the horses, we kept seeing a blue mustang drive up and down the road, driving a little too fast at times, then slowed down to a stop, to look at a piece of paper. You see, Dawn, bet me if he had blue eyes and a hairy chest that I had to go out with him. If he didn't, she'd buy my lunch. She is always fixing me up on blind dates. Anyway, she was awfully anxious for me to see what this guy looked like."

"Oh, my wife didn't pass away. We had got divorced and she moved out. Rumor has it that she ran off with Sofia's ex-husband. And that's why...never mind. So did Dawn know who he was?"

"Apparently it is Dr. Viza, Michael. He is her husband's best friend. They are as close as Dawn and I are. He recently moved from Texas. Dawn invited him to look at the house that day, and for us to meet."

"Okay, so how did you have your accident?"

"I wasn't too happy with her when I found out she was trying to hook me up again and I took off racing Abraham back up to the barn. A black snake slithered across the grass and it spooked Abraham, making him rare up, bucking me off. According to Dawn, he came driving up and ran to my side. He's the one who picked me up and drove me to the hospital."

"Is that right? Dr. Viza might be a pretty good catch, Michelle. At least he has money. You'd be in good care since he's a doctor."

Jesse didn't miss a beat, covering up any jealousy tendencies he was feeling.

"Barbie, my granddaughter has a lot of respect for him. In fact, I think she'd like to date him. He asked her out for dinner this week."

"Really, well tell her to go for it, because I'm not interested in the least. He seemed too, ugh, occupied or something. Maybe if it works out for them, Dawn will leave me alone and stop fixing me up."

"Are you sure you don't mind Barbie going out with him? And how come you don't want Dawn fixing you up with anyone?"

"That makes anyone look desperate. I don't like blind dates because they are awkward and normally don't work out. So why would I mind if Barbie wants to go out with him? I wish her well with him."

They both were looking at one another, silence filling the air.

"What were you going to say about your neighbor why she...what?"

"It's not important Michelle. Don't worry your pretty head over it."

"Jesse, you know I have had feelings for you for quite some time now. And that is the very reason I haven't got married to anyone. I was waiting for you, preferably, or someone like you, that had your sexy charm and good qualities."

Jesse laugh filled the air.

"I finally realized there is no one out there that could possibly fill your shoes and make me feel the way I do when I am with you. God made only one Jesse Lee Fox. God broke the mold when He made you. Dawn always tells me that every guy I ever dated, I'd compare him to you and if they didn't measure up, which they never came close, I dump him."

Jesse was looking at Michelle with amusement.

"Oh, my precious Michelle. Just what am I going to do with you?"

"I remember you asking me that in high school once, and I still don't know the answer to that. Do you?"

He took her hand into his nice warm hands, smile and wink at her.

"So Jess, just what are you going to do with me? I'd love to know."

"You would, huh?"

"Yes, I would very much so. I've waited so long Jesse, to hear it from you."

He would bring her hand to his lips and kiss the back of her hand gently.

"Michelle, you must know, or have some inkling of an idea of how I feel about you, don't you?"

"No, I don't, not really. You have never verbally expressed it to me. You have always been nice to me, but as far as how you truly feel, no, I can't say that I do. I've always hoped you had the same feelings for me as I do for you. I have fantasized about you so often throughout the years; I've actually cried myself to sleep."

"I'm sorry babe."

"So that's when I started writing love letters to you and shared my fantasies I had, hoping that I would get a reply back, but never did. Guess I will never know, huh?"

"Never say never, my love."

"Yea, okay, whatever."

"I'm here now, aren't I?"

Michelle didn't respond. Jesse leaned forward, pulling Michelle closer. When they were inches apart, he lightly kissed her lips. Michelle deeply exhaled, shutting her eyes. She opened them to look into Jesse's deep, dark chocolate brown eyes she thought were always so beautiful. Jesse kissed her again, parting his lips and briefly touching her soft lips before he pulled away.

"And how about now, sweetheart?" All Michelle could do was smile, taking a deep breath. Jesse winked at her, making her smile that much more.

"We should get something for lunch and watch a movie. How does that sound?'" Jesse asked her.

"I'll be right back. Does chicken sound alright?"

"From Lane's?"

"No, hopefully, better than that. I actually fried some this morning, after my electricity came back on, intending to bring it over, hoping you agreed to have lunch with me. That's why I called."

"Oh really? Wow, Jesse! I didn't even know you knew how to cook."

"There are some things you don't know about me, which might take you by surprise."

"Really? Hmmm..., do tell. I'd love to hear them. Actually, I'd love to hear everything about you."

"All in due time, my love. All in due time."

"Since I didn't fix anything but fried chicken, I did go by Lane's and pick up some sides. I hope you like baked beans, corn on the cob and fried okra?"

"Jesse, they are all my favorites. How did you know?"

Jesse got up from the sofa smiling, and then went outside to his car to bring in food. Michelle got up and hobbled to the kitchen. Jesse came in bringing a couple of sacks.

"What are you doing on that ankle young lady? I knew I'd better come over and start taking care of you."

Jesse went into the kitchen where Michelle was and reached for a couple of glasses from the cabinet that Michelle started reaching for. And then he took out a couple of plates and found the silverware. He then put some ice in the glasses and started bringing the plates and glasses into the dining room, sitting them on the table.

"Thank you."

"No problem. Now get off that ankle before I whip you."

Michelle sat down at the dining room table. Jesse took the food out of the bags as Michelle watched him. He pulled out a bottle of Pepsi and Dr. Pepper.

"All we need now is the food on our plates and our glasses filled. Dark or white meat?"

"Dark please."

Jesse put a thigh on her plate.

"Okay, now what? A little of beans, corn cob, and okra?"

"Yes please and thank you, but Jess, I can fix my own plate."

"Hush and don't fuss. Let me take care of you sweetheart. I got Pepsi and Dr. Pepper, as you can tell. I remember you used to drink Pepsi, but I think you switched on me your senior year, to this other stuff. Am I correct?"

"Yes, wow, I can't believe you remember that. You used to call me your Pepsi girl."

Yea, then you go and turned on me. I think you need a whipping for that too." Michelle started laughing. Jesse finished serving Michelle and then started fixing his plate.

"Jesse, I'd like to pray over the food first, before we start eating. Do you mind?"

"Don't trust my cooking eh?" Just kidding. No, go ahead. I think it's a good idea."

Michelle smiled and took his hand in hers and started praying, thanking God for the food, asking Him to bless the hands that prepared it and to bless their fellowship together.

"In Jesus name, amen."

"Amen. that was beautiful Michelle. Thank you. Guess you won't be afraid to eat my cooking now." Jesse teased.

"Nope. Not now," she teased back.

"Seriously, I do pray over my food, when I don't forget."

Michelle took a bite of her chicken. Mm...Jess, this is delicious. Where on earth did you learn how to cook chicken this juicy and tender?

"My grandmother taught me. I had watched her cook growing up, over the years. Then one day she let me help her. She was careful to teach me right in everything, not just cooking. She was a good Christian lady. I can still hear her say:"

Jesse imitated an old grandma's voice and was pointing and shaking his finger.

"Now Jesse, not too much oil or it will be too greasy. But not too little either or it will be too dry and burn. But just enough to make it juicy. You know honey, a way to a man's heart is through his stomach, but that also goes for women. Awe, I'd do cartwheels if your grandpa knew how to cook for me. Sometimes, a lady needs a break, you know what I mean Jess?"

"Yea, she was something else. I miss her a lot."

"How long ago did she pass away?"

"Seven years ago. She was 97. She lived a long fruitful life."

"I'm sorry Jesse. I wished I could have met her."

"Thank you, love. Me too."

"So, do you have any pets, Michelle"?

"No, not any of my own. Just the Macafey's horses in the barn. Why do you ask? Do you have any animals?"

"No, I don't. The reason why I was asking is that my friend's dog is having puppies and I told him I'd help get rid of them."

"Oh, what kind are they?"

"Not actually sure. The mother is a St. Bernard."

"Awe, that's my favorite dog, well one of them. I have several. I like Golden Retrievers too. As for small, dogs, I like Shi-Tzu's."

"I really don't have a favorite really. They all require time and attention, potty-training them, feeding them, health care. You know, kinda like children."

"So, you'd prefer not to have any animals, is that what you're saying Jes?"

"No, I didn't say that honey. A person gets attached to animals more than they realize. They become a part of the family, and when anything happens to them, it hurts, you know?"

"Yes, I definitely know what you mean. Especially if you are an animal lover like I am."

"Are you just an animal lover?" Jesse reached over and put his warm hand on Michelle's. They looked into one another's eyes. She was thinking about what Dawn told her.

"Michelle babe, what is it? Did I say something wrong?"

"No, no. It's nothing. I'm just...ugh could you pass me another biscuit please?"

"Sure." and Jesse buttered it and squeezed honey on it like she did her first one and handed it to her.

"Thank you. You are so thoughtful Jess."

"I try to be. No need in being any other way, is there?"

"No, not at all. It was just that I was thinking about what Dawn had told me earlier."

"Oh no. What was that? That I am some kind of Psycho maniac or something?" Michelle started laughing.

"Well, not in so many words. Besides, I know better than that."

"I hope so. There is nothing that I wouldn't do for you, Michelle. I want you to know that."

He looked at her lovingly.

"Thank you."

"Babe, please don't be so suspicious. You were always curious, paranoid, little girl but was a very cute and smart girl in school, who I happened to fall in love with back then."

Michelle studied him, looking into his beautiful deep dark brown eyes, realizing what he just confessed to her. That he fell in love with her back then.

"Paranoid huh? There were many times after I graduated high school, that I'd get a funny feeling I was being followed or being ugh, supervised if you will. Or different people cross my path and I felt as if they knew you, for some reason. Maybe you were sending them in the grocery store to check up on me or whatever. Was my "paranoia ", correct? Will you be honest and tell me that, please?"

Michelle was so serious with curiosity, tilting her head to one side, looking into his beautiful brown eyes she loved so much.

"Oh Michelle, my precious love. All you need to know right now is that I fell hard, truly, madly, deeply in love with you many years ago. It was love at first sight. Please believe me, and trust me when I tell you that I love you with all my heart and soul. If I told you anymore right now, you'd get so mad at me. I'm afraid you wouldn't ever want to see me again. So, on that note, let's keep this light and simple and enjoy our time together, please? It's been so long, Michelle. I can't tell you how many times I've longed for us to be together like this."

Jesse looked into her mysterious, pretty hazel cat eyes with sincerity. She wasn't expecting that kind of answer at all. She was shocked by what he did tell her, but he still didn't answer her question. Just another mind game he was playing with her as he did in high school. However, this time she believed he'd tell her everything in due time. At least he didn't deny anything she asked him. Jesse touched her hand, bringing it up to his lips to kiss it. Michelle finally smiled at him then. He was so relieved she was satisfied with that answer.

"This was a great meal Jess, especially the okra."

She started laughing.

"I'll remember that the next time you want some more of my chicken."

"No, no, don't. I'm sorry. I was only kidding. I'm sorry."

He was laughing too, getting up from the table, clearing their plates and taking them into the kitchen.

"Jesse, please. You don't have to clean up. I'll get to it later. It will give me something to do."

"You are not to be on your ankle young lady. End of story. It won't take me long but a few minutes, and I will be back by your side. Perhaps, we can watch a movie?"

Michelle hobbled to the front door and look out to see if it was still raining. "Well, it has stopped raining and the sun is shining again."

He looked out the kitchen window as he was washing the dishes. As he finished washing the plates and silverware, he came up behind Michelle and kissed her on her neck and whisper in her ear.

"I bet the sun came back out when you finally smiled at me, from our conversation earlier. You were so serious before and looked like you were mad or angry with me. And I bet when you smiled at me, that's when it stopped raining and the sun came out."

"Oh Jesse, stop it."

They came back into the living room and sat down on the sofa. As they were sitting down on the sofa, and him still holding her hand, he lifted it to his lips again and kissed it, watching her response. She closed her eyes, smiling, then looked at him. She leaned over just enough to let him know she wanted a kiss. He didn't hesitate as he leaned in and fulfilled her wish. Her wish was his every command. He gently put his arm around her and pulled her closer to softly graze her lips. Michelle let out a soft breath, letting him know she wanted a real kiss. This time, he took her lips into his, kissing top, then bottom separately, before he kissed her fully. For a moment, Michelle felt no pain in her ankle whatsoever and felt like she was floating to a place she's never been. His kiss was so gentle, but with passion. He pulled away slowly, ending it as he started it as if to seal his kiss with a kiss.

Michelle hugged him, for a long time before she pulled away. His eyes seemed to hypnotize her, drawing her in. She caught him by surprise and winked at him, smiling. He'd smile back at her and wink back. But when she tried to wink at him again, she blinked both of her eyes, making him laugh, which made her laugh as well. He hugged her and then leaned back onto the sofa, pulling her with him.

"So what's on your agenda for today, Ms. Michelle?"

"Oh, not a whole lot. I imagine I will write some on my second novel, putting the finishing touches to it so I can fax it to my publisher tonight."

"Second book?"

"Yea, my first one has been published for a while now. I'm hoping it will become a best seller and turn into a movie."

"Wow! Really? Isn't that something? I had no idea love. That is fantastic! Congratulations! Do you think your second book will become a movie too?"

"I'm certainly hoping so, but let's not count the chickens before they hatch Jess. Prayerfully it will."

"Well, maybe it will. We can always hope. I have all the confidence in the world in you Michelle. I always have. It will be your second #1 best seller."

"I love the way you always have encouraged me to do my best. Thank you for that. But if it does, it'd be all God doing it, certainly not me. That's for sure. He is the one who deserves all the credit."

"Well, He gave you the desire to write, so, He must have given you the talent."

"You're absolutely right. I have all the confidence in Him, to, let this happen for me. Before I started writing my first book, and my second, I asked God to help, lead and guide me in writing it, to help me minister to the ones who need it at the right time in their lives."

"You have a lot of faith Michelle. I can tell you love God with all your heart and soul."

"Thank you. You are helping me to increase my faith and confidence, with your encouragement you give me. You did that in school for me too. This was one of the many things I love about you. God must have put you in my life because He knew I needed all the encouragement and confidence I could get. Especially concerning my books getting published and made into movies. It has been one of my biggest dreams."

She brought Jesse's hand to her lips and kissed it.

"And you, Mr. Jesse Lee Fox, is the other biggest dream, which has come true so far."

Jesse took delight in what she said and smiled at her.

"I am so glad you feel that way, my love. You have been good for me too, and have helped me out a lot, over the years. You have no idea how much you've helped me too. I can't begin to tell you how you've helped me. You have shown confidence and faith in me, in different things as well. And I want to thank you for that. I don't know what I'd have done without you in those times. I can't begin to repay you for everything you mean to me Michelle, but I intend to do my ever loving best to try."

Jesse kissed her hand and squeezed it.

"Only if you will let me?"

Michelle leaned in to kiss him lovingly.

"Yes My Darling, I am more than willing to let you."

Michelle flipped on the TV and they found a movie they both agreed on and watched it from beginning to end.

Chapter Six

*J*esse looked at his watch.

"I better run off so you can finish your second number one best seller. I need to clean the house before the guys come over. One of the guys I work with is getting married next Saturday and we are throwing him a bachelor party. So I need to tidy up a little and go to the store and get a few things to snack on."

"Sounds like fun, but don't party too much."

"Oh no, I won't. The guys probably will, and that's why I suggested it be at my house, so if they do party too much, they can crash at my place."

"Good. If I were you, I'd have a bowl at the door to put their car keys in, and then hide them when they weren't looking."

Jesse starts to laugh.

"Not a bad idea Michelle. I just might do that. Thanks!"

Jesse stood up and leaned over to kiss her on the cheek. Jesse walked into the kitchen to wash his glass and put it on the counter. She was at the door, waiting to see him out.

"Didn't I say to stay off that ankle young lady?"

Michelle put her hand on his chest, sliding it up to his face. Jesse took it and kissed the inside of her palm, then took her into his arms, kissing her passionately. He picked her up and carried her back to the sofa.

"Now, where is your laptop?"

"Down the hall, to your right. It's sitting on the desk, Jess."

He found it and brought it to her.

"Now, Ms. Independent, stay off your ankle, keep it propped up on the table with this pillow, and type away. Get some rest in between and don't work too hard. I will call you later. Need a refill of Dr. Pepper?"

"Please?"

"Sure thing. Coming right up."

He took her empty glass and refilled it with ice and more soda, bringing it back to her, giving her one last kiss goodbye.

"I'll talk to you soon babe. I love you. Keep plugging away on your book. Stay off your ankle."

And Jesse was out the door. A few hours later and Michelle completed her manuscript and then e-mailed it to the publisher.

A few days passed by without a word from Jesse, and she was feeling a little down. Her ankle was healing quite nicely and she could put her weight on it without hurting it. She walked out to the mailbox to check the mail to find three magazines, a couple of bills, and a letter from the Macafey's. When she came back up to the porch, she noticed a pretty red rose laying on the porch swing with a card. It brought a smile to her lips, knowing it must be from Jesse. She went over, sat down on the swing, picked up the beautiful red rose smelling it and opened the card. She noticed the card smelled of Jesse's cologne and the rose smelled so fresh and rosy. The card read:

My Precious Michelle Love,

I hope you can find it in your heart to forgive me, that I haven't called you lately. But some things came up that I can't get into right now, but promise to explain to you at a later time. I will be calling you soon Babe. I have missed you.

All my love,
Jesse

P.S. I watched that TV preacher you wanted me to watch. I liked him. He's alright. Thank you for telling me about him. I will be talking to you very soon, My Love. I hope you enjoy the rose, and your ankle is much better. See you soon.

Xoxo ;-)

Michelle was so happy to finally hear from Jesse she was beaming from ear to ear. She smelled the rose and the card again and opened up the other mail. When she opened the letter from the Macafey's, there were three checks. One was for the water bill she opened already, the second check was written to PSO and the other check was for her. The letter was a thank you letter for taking care of their place while they were gone and letting her know they'd be coming home in a few days if things went as well as they have been. Michelle's mood instantly perked up since she finally heard from her Jesse. It was a beautiful spring day after all. Her ankle was feeling much better and walking without her crutches. She went inside and laid the mail down on the dining room table before she sat down and then paid the water bill and PSO with the checks the Mcafeys sent, After she sealed the envelope, her phone rang.

"Hello?"

"Hi Michelle, how are you feeling? This is Pastor Chip. We have been missing you, young lady."

"Hi, Pastor! Thanks for calling. My ankle is doing much better. I can walk without crutches now. It doesn't hurt anymore. I have been staying off of it and keeping it up like everyone has told me to do. How's church been? A lot of people been coming?"

"We had 112 there this past Sunday and 74 there on Wednesday!" But it was our potluck night."

"Really, still that is good for a Wednesday night Pastor. Garfield"

"Well, Sister Joanna and I just wanted to call and check on you. So glad to hear you are feeling better. Your Sunday school kids have missed you. Britney has been filling in for you while you been gone."

"I will be sure and give her a call and tell her thank you. Tell Sister Joanna, your better half that I said hi and give her a hug for me and tell her I love her. I love you too Pastor. Y'all are the greatest Pastors I've ever had."

"Hi sister Michelle. I'm here. How's it going? I love you too. Get back to church. We miss you."

"Michelle, we are the only Pastors you've had., and Ill have to agree with you that she is my better half."

"I know, that's why y'all are the greatest!"

"Oh, Michelle. Be good, okay. See you Sunday."

"Okay Pastors, thanks for calling. Have a blessed day."

Michelle turned on some christian music to play from her phone before she started cleaning. Michelle started laundry; cleaned the kitchen, washing the few dishes that were in the sink. After she cleaned the guest bathroom, she went and started cleaning her bathroom before her cell phone rang. She didn't recognize the number.

"Hello?"

"Hello, Michelle. It's been a while; do you know who this is?"

"I'm sorry. Who is this?"

"Remember you made me the best lasagna that I've ever tasted in my life."

There was a brief pause.

"Randy? Randy, is that you? Oh my gosh! How are you?"

He started laughing.

"Well, it depends on how many other guys you fixed lasagna for. Yes, it's me. How are you?"

"Great! And as for that lasagna, my first time of making it, I'm sure you have tasted much better since then, I hope anyway."

"No, no it WAS good."

"Ok, whatever! Hey, how's your little girl, Stacy? I bet she has grown up to be a fine young lady."

"Oh yeah, she's twelve now, going on thirty-three. She has her first boyfriend already."

"I can't believe dad let her have one of those. Is there wedding bells in the future?"

"Oh no, we are not going there. My little Stacy isn't going to get married."

"Oh, yea she will dad. But in the meantime, she will break plenty of hearts."

"Michelle, I was wondering if you'd like to go out sometime soon."

"Ugh".

"You know, just to catch up on old times. Have dinner and a movie night?" Michelle was receiving another call on the other line.

"Randy, I'm sorry, I am getting another call. I'll think about it and give you a call back. Is this your cell phone number?

"Yes, it's the only phone I have."

"Ok, Bye. I'll let you know."

Michelle switched over to her other call.

"Hello?"

"Hello, Beautiful. How's my sugar baby doing?"

Michelle instantly knew it was her Jesse and a huge smile came across her lips.

"Hi,. Goodlookin! It's about time you call me. Where have you been?"

"Oh, there is time for that. How's my Love doing? How's your ankle? All better, I hope?"

"Yea, I can actually walk on it without the crutches and hurting."

"You still should be careful babe. Have you gone back to Dr. Viza yet?"

"No."

"Maybe you should have him check it over. Maybe you could get your cast off, you think?"

"Yea, maybe. The missionaries are coming back in a few days. It'd be great if I was out of the cast before they arrive."

"Why don't I pick you up and we go to the hospital. Barbie doesn't even know I'm back yet."

"Speaking of which, where have you been Jesse?"

"Just out of pocket a few days. I will tell you later."

"Promise?"

"Cross my heart."

"Ok, I am going to hold you to that."

"I look forward to it. I've missed you, Michelle. I also look forward to holding you in my arms and kissing you again."

"Awe...you missed me, huh?"

"Sure did."

"Well, let's hang the phone up so you can get over here."

There was an instant silence on the phone.

"Jesse?"

Michelle looked at her cell phone and it said call ended. When she turned around and looked out the front door, Jesse was getting out of his black Cadillac. Michelle was amazed how Jesse could still put butterflies in her stomach. She has loved him for a very long time and just couldn't believe he was back in her life. She was feeling like a schoolgirl again. She walked out onto the front porch as he walked up the steps by two and onto the porch, wrapping his arms around her, giving her a big hug. He held her for a long time.

"Hi Beautiful. Aren't you a sight for sore eyes?"

He pulled away from her and looked at her."

"Oh Jesse, I have missed you something crazy. Thought you dropped off the face of the earth."

He laughed.

"No Darlin. I'm here Babe. I'm here."

He put his hand behind her neck and pulled her lips to his to kiss her fully. It took Michelle's breath away and she pulled away to catch her breath. After she composed herself, she moved in to give him a kiss.

They pulled away from one another and Michelle got ready to go to the hospital with Jesse.

"Do I need to carry you down the steps Love?"

"No, I'll make it. Thanks though "

"Be careful."

Michelle made it down the steps with Jesse right beside her for support. He opens the car door for her, helping her get in the car and then got in on the other side and they headed for the hospital. Dr. Viza took the cast off, X-rayed it and put a boot on instead of a cast and told her to come back in a couple weeks, which it was healing quite nicely. When Barbie was finished with her shift, she saw Jesse and Michelle waiting for her at the nurse's station.

"Grandpa! You made it back! How was your trip?"

"Hi sweetheart. It went well."

They hugged briefly.

"Hi Michelle. I see your cast is off. That's good!"

"Yea, I am happy about that. A couple more weeks, and Dr. Viza said this boot will come off too."

"That's great!"

"Sweetheart, Michelle and I were going home but was going to get a bite to eat somewhere. Would you like to join us?"

"Awe, no I'm sorry. Michael and I made plans. May I take a rain check?"

"Michael? You mean, Dr. Viza? Where is he taking you, if you don't mind me asking?"

"Yes, Dr. Viza. There is a band that's playing somewhere that he enjoys hearing and asked me to join him."

"Ok, be careful. Have fun."

Jesse and Michelle left the hospital and drove through Taco Barn to get a couple burrito and taco platters and went back to Jesse's house. When they drove up, Jesse's neighbor was outside watering her flowers.

"Uh oh." Jesse muttered under his breath.

"What was that Jess?" Michelle asked, looking at him.

"Oh it's nothing."

"Jesse, you have a nice house. It looks very nice out front here. I love your pretty flowers in the flower bed and around the tree there."

"Thanks. My wife planted all of them. I don't have a green thumb. She was the gardener around here."

They walked up to his front door as Sofia, Jesse's neighbor waved at them and started walking over to chat, like Jesse knew she would do but hoped she wouldn't. Sofia was tall, slender, with a dark tan. She had long, wavy coal black hair that came down to her waist.

"Hey neighbor. Where have you been? I hadn't seen you in a while. Who's your friend?"

"Hi Sophia. This is my good friend Michelle. Listen, I hadn't been home, like you know and I am just now getting back. Will you please excuse us?"

Sophia looked at him in haste and scoffed off. Michelle couldn't help but grin, feeling very happy that Jesse shooed her off. This must have been the neighbor that she heard on the phone the other day.

They walked in his house as Jesse walked to the kitchen.

"I like your house Jess. Very nice."

"Well thank you. It's been a good little house, even been through the tornado that one year, but after the remodel, she was as good as new again."

"Yea, I remember that tornado. It was crazy!"

"Yes, yes it was that alright. Make yourself at home. My casa, your casa."

Michelle sat down at his kitchen table as Jesse was getting a couple plates to put their food on.

"Shall we eat in the living room, or out on the back patio?"

"I will follow you. It doesn't make any difference to me."

Jesse would walk to his back door and slide it open. He had a cute little table for two with two chairs. They ate their lunch and enjoyed each other's company, until they saw Sophia out in her backyard, mowing in her two piece bikini.

Michelle caught Jesse watching Sophia as he would look back at Michelle. "What?"

"I can't believe you Jesse. Do you have feelings for her?"

"No babe, I don't. Honest."

"Then why are you watching her? I was having a lovely afternoon but I believe it's time for me to leave now. Please take me home."

"Sweetheart, please don't do this."

"Well, I don't want to keep you. Obviously, you have other things on your mind."

''Michelle...''

Michelle just shook her head in dismay, looking away from Jesse as she stood up and went back into his house. Jesse finished eating his taxo, wiped his mouth with a napkin and went to ho find Michelle. He found her in the living room, looking at all his family pictures on the walls. When Jesse walked in the living room, Michelle spoke first.

"Jesse, I want to ask you something."

"What is it Love?'

"Back when I was in high school and during lunch, I remember you watching me for the longest time one day. What was going through your mind? That has crossed my mind several times and wished I hadn't been so dog gone shy back then or I would have asked you then."

Jesse recalled that particular day. He remembered because he had just found out his brother had just passed away and that his wife had left him because of a fight they had.

"Come here. I want to take you on a tour of the house."

"Jesse, you didn't answer my question."

"Honey, I've slept since then. How do you expect me to remember what I was thinking years ago? I can barely remember what happened yesterday."

"Uh huh, right Jesse Lee Fox. You remember. You just don't want to tell me."

"Are you calling me a liar Michelle Renee' Mertz?"

"Yes, yes I am because I can tell when you are lying."

"Oh, is that so, huh?"

"Yes"

"If you must know, I was thinking all sorts of things, but mostly, wishing my circumstances were different and that you and I could have been together way back then."

Jesse took her hand in his, kissing it and they walked through his cute little 3 bedrooms, 2 bathrooms house.

"You have a cute house, Jesse. Is it paid for?"

"Yes, it is."

Jesse was watching Michelle as she was looking at his pictures in the hall and came up behind her, sliding his arms around her, whispering in her ear.

"A Garfield for your thoughts."

"I was just thinking, if the circumstances were different back then, and we had hooked up after I had graduated and had married, what our children would have looked like."

Michelle closed her eyes as he started kissing her on her neck. She leaned against him, desiring more. Jesse turned her around and kissed her passionately.

"I bet they would have looked like their beautiful mother. Stay a little bit longer Michelle, please?"

"Jesse, Dr. Viza released me to go back to work tomorrow."

"Yes, but he also said it didn't mean you had to go back tomorrow, that you could go back on Monday."

He kissed her on her neck again and pulled her closer to him slowly.

"Jess, please...stop." He pulled away and gave her a quick kiss on the cheek.

"Ok, your wish is my command my love. I'm sorry. It's just that you really are addictive."

Michelle started laughing.

"Awe...thank you."

Jesse took her home and walked her up to her front door.

"So, you're going back to work tomorrow then?"

"Yes. I work from 9a.m. to 3p.m. Sandy called me and asked if I'd work for her and I said I would."

"Well, don't work too hard pretty lady."

"I won't."

Michelle was still ticked at Jesse for watching Sophia, in her slutty, itsy, bitsy pink bikini, with her long black wavy hair flowing down to her waist, long slender tanned legs with painted bright pink long fake nails. Her toe nails painted the same color as her fingernails. The more she thought about her and the more she thought about Jesse watching her, the angrier she was getting. Michelle watched Jesse drive away before she called Dawn.

"Dawn, you know how we had talked about going into the private eye business? Well, tonight we have our chance. Get over here as fast as you can, and wear dark clothes."

"What's going on Michelle?"

"Oooo, I'm so pissed right now! I think Jesse is lying to me! And I want to catch him."

"Why, what happened?"

"Please hurry."

Chapter Seven

*M*ichelle ended their call and Dawn was over there in minutes. Michelle told Dawn everything that happened as they drove over to Jesse's but parked a little way down the street so as not to tip him off. It was around 9:30 in the evening, on a cloudy June day.

"What are we going to do?"

"Let's just wait and watch right now. I honestly can't stand that Sophia. She sure knows how to get Jesse's attention."

They watched Jesse's house for a few minutes and then they saw Sophia walking over to Jesse's front door carrying a bottle of red wine.

"Are you freaking kidding me!? She just struts on in like she lives there!"

"So, what's the plan? Are we going to...?"

"I don't know exactly, but let's walk up there and look through his windows."

Michelle and Dawn get out of Dawn's SUV and they walked up to Jesse's, being careful not to get caught. It was completely dark so that helped. They walked to the side of his house to look through his living room window. Jesse had opened up his window to let the breeze come in. Sophia was pouring them a glass of red wine and Jesse was nowhere to be seen.

"I wonder where he is, and what's that?"

Dawn whispered, pointing to a massage table that wasn't there before now. Michelle put her finger to her lips telling her to "Shhh". Just then, Jesse came out from down the hall, wrapped in a towel, and his hair wet. Michelle could see water glistening on his chest, from his shower. Sophia was now wearing a slinky multi-colored sun-dress with spaghetti straps and a slit on the side going up to her thigh.

"What are you doing Sophia?"

"I thought we could have a nightcap together. I've really missed you Studly."

"Sophia look, I'm really beat.. It's been a very long day."

"Let me give you a relaxing massage while you drink your wine I poured for you."

She handed him his glass of wine, clinked her glass with his and said cheers. He took a drink of his wine and she took a drink of hers, then she took his hand and led him to the massaging table she evidently set up earlier, while he was taking a shower.

"I'm not taking no for an answer Jess. Now lay down here and let me put some massaging oil on you that will help you relax, preferably without the towel."

She giggled like a schoolgirl as Jesse looked at her with a half assed grin. Michelle was fuming at this point. Dawn calmed her down a bit as they continued to watch Sophia. Dawn showed Michelle that she was using her phone to video tape them, with audio. Jesse was too tired to fight with her and laid down on the table.

"Good boy. Now, before I get started, let's play some music."

Sophia took her cell phone and scrolled through it. When she laid it down on the table, it started playing Bad Boy by Cascadia.

"Oh, how appropriate." Michelle whispered.

Sophia put the oil on her hands first and then started rubbing her hands all over his back. Michelle could tell Jesse was enjoying it by his soft groans.

"I can't do this."

Michelle growled. Dawn took Michelle's wrist and led her away from the window so she could talk to her.

"Michelle, this is your chance to catch him, her, them. Hell, I really want to catch him for the way he raked me and Michael over the coals."

"Okay. Wait, what?"

"I will tell you about it later."

"Dawn, why is he letting her do this?"

"I don't know, but my phone does pretty good videos. It's all being caught on my phone, whatever is going on now. Let's get back."

When they returned, they saw Jesse's wine glass empty as was Sophia's. She was sitting straddling Jesse, facing him. He was facing her, watching her, still laying down on the massage table. She bent down and kissed him on the lips. Jesse was just lying there, letting her do whatever she wanted to him. Michelle and Dawn continued to watch this charade until Jesse finally sat up and Sophia got off him. Michelle was thankful Jesse still had his towel on.

"Sophia, I'm not feeling well. My head is spinning"

"Oh, you will be okay. You're probably just relaxed now. Let's dance. I love this song." Sexual Healing was playing and so Sophia took him in her arms and they started dancing. She started kissing Jesse, and then Jesse laid his head on her shoulder. Michelle was livid at this point. After the song was over, Sophia led him down the hall into his bedroom.

Michelle ran to Dawn's car and got in, screaming loudly. Before Dawn went to the car, she walked around outside his house to see if she could see into his bedroom. When she approached his bedroom window, his bedside lamp was on a low dim and Dawn watched Sophia pull down her spaghetti straps revealing her bare breasts as Jesse was lying on his bed watching her. Sophia was standing in front of him, blocking his bare middle section. Dawn saw his towel he had on earlier, now on the floor. Sophia climbed on top of him again. Dawn had seen enough and walked back to her car, but she was able to also capture this on her phone, recording it for Michelle.

The next morning, Michelle got up and got ready for work. She left the house and arrived right on time. The day started off slow, and then picked up around noon time. She was working in the customer service booth cashing payroll checks, counting down tills, and cashiering when it got busy. When she went on break, she noticed Jesse and Dawn left her voice messages.

"Hello Love, I hope your day is going well and not working too hard. I'd like to take you out to dinner tonight, if you don't have any prior engagements. Let me know."

Michelle was beyond furious with him and didn't call him back. Michelle listened to Dawn's message.

"Sis, I finally got my video to play from last night. I guess it needed charged. Anyway, after reviewing what I had recorded, I believe it's not entirely Jesse's fault what took place last night, as much as I hate to admit it. Call me."

Michelle finished her break and went back to work. The rest of her shift went by quickly since it was busy and she cashiered the remainder of her shift. She took her cell phone out, walking to her car and called Dawn back.

"Hey Dawn, so this has got to be good, if you are taking up for Jesse."

"Can you come over? You won't believe it otherwise."

"Yea, I just got off work. I'll be there in a few minutes. Jesse wants to take me out to dinner tonight. He left a message."

"If I were you, I wouldn't. But that's up to you."

Michelle arrived at Dawn's house and Danielle came running up to Michelle with delight, as Michelle picked her up and kissed her.

"Hi Aunt Shell. Are you having snack time with us? Mommy made some no bake cookies."

"Mmmmmm, they are your mom's and I's favorite cookie."

"I know, mine too!"

"Where's Jacob?"

"He and daddy went fishing."

They walked in Dawn's house as Dawn was taking out a pan of cookies out of the refrigerator and started putting them on a plate.

"How's my favorite girl doing?"

Michelle sat down with Danielle in her lap, giving her kisses.

Danielle giggled.

"Fine."

"Sweetheart, why don't you go find your new favorite toy that daddy bought you the other day."

"Okay mommy. I'll be right back Aunt Shell."

She jumped down off Michelle's lap. running down the hall into her bedroom and Dawn gave Michelle her cell phone to watch the video from last night.

Sophia had put something in Jesse's wine.

"So that's why he felt sick. That Bi...!"

Danielle came running back to Michelle, pulling a toy behind her.

"Here it is Aunt Shell. See! It's a talking and walking dog."

"I see. How cool!"

Dawn poured her daughter a glass of milk and put a couple cookies on a plate.

"Sis, do you want a glass of milk with your cookies?"

"Sure."

Dawn poured Michelle and herself a glass of milk, putting a plate of cookies on the table.

Danielle ate her two cookies and finished her milk, and then ran off to play with her new toy.

Michelle looked at Dawn, shaking her head.

"I can't believe that bitch. What should I do Dawn?"

"Oh I don't know. Catch her in a dark alley somewhere and beat her to a pulp."

"Don't tempt me. Ugh! I can't believe her! Or him! I wonder what she put in his drink."

"Probably the date-rape drug, because that's what she did."

Michelle looked at Dawn's clock on the wall. It was 3:57 p.m.

"Jesse's probably wondering where I am. He sounded pretty chipper on the phone when he left me that message. He must have been out of his mind, letting that slut Sofia sink her claws into him!"

"Michelle, he may not even remember what happened. Go easy on him."

"I'm really surprised to hear you say that."

"Well, honestly, I don't believe Mr. Fox would be unfaithful to you."

"Why do you say that?"

"Because of what he said to Michael and me."

"Oh yea, I was going to ask you about that. What are you talking about him talking to you and Michael? I'm confused."

Michelle's cell phone started ringing and it was Jesse. Hesitantly, Michelle answered. "Hello."

"Hi Love. I thought you'd be home by now. Where are you?"

"I'm at Dawn's."

"Oh, everything okay?"

There was a pause.

"Michelle?"

"Jesse"

"Honey, what it is? You sound mad. Are you okay?"

"Yes, I'm fine. I'll see you in a little while. Bye Jesse."

Michelle cut the call short.

"I will text you the video and you can do what you want."

"Ok sis. Thanks. So what did Jesse talk to you and Dr. Viza about?"

"It's crazy. I'll tell you about it some other time. But I will tell you that Mr. Fox doesn't believe in fidelity."

"Ok, tell me as soon as you can. I'm really intrigued now. I guess I better go or he will be over here, checking up on me!"

Chapter Eight

When Michelle arrived home, she saw the Macafey's car and Jesse's car but they were nowhere to be found. Michelle got out of her car and walked up to the patio and went inside. A few minutes went by and she heard the Macafey's voices and then Jesse's, coming up on the porch and walked in.

"Well, this is a pleasant surprise! How are you two? Looks like you met Jesse."

"Oh dear. He is such a fine young man."

Grace walked over and hugged Michelle as George and Jesse were still chatting about the good ole days back when George was in the cotton fields.

"How was your flight back Grace?"

"Oh it was long, but nice. It's good to be on solid ground again. We got in about 2 p.m. I think it was. We didn't know who was driving up shortly after we got home so we both walked outside to investigate. Jesse explained who he was and asked about the land, horses, and house. I'm sorry deer, to hear Abraham throwing you off. Are you feeling better?"

"Oh yea. Much, thank you."

"George, get in here and greet Michelle properly. You been talking poor Jesse's ear off for the past thirty minutes or longer."

Michelle started laughing as George and Jesse walked in the kitchen. George gave her a hug.

"How you doing Michelle? How's your ankle?"

"Oh it's alright. Much better than it was. Thank you for asking. How are you? How's Hon Dourous?"

"Oh let me tell you, them people are so hungry for God's word. We have a full house every service."

"Well that's great news!"

"We better let these kids get ready for their evening out. It was so nice to meet you Jesse."

"The pleasure is all mine, Grace, George."

He shook their hands firmly and followed Michelle into the living room.

"How was your first day back to work Babe?", as Jesse took her into his arms, looking at her lovingly.

"Not too bad. Busy, which made it go faster. How was your day?"

"Other than missing you like crazy, it went well I reckon."

They kissed briefly and Michelle exited, going to her room and freshen up for their evening out. She forgot to ask Jesse what to wear, so she poked her head out and hollered for him to come to her bedroom. He answered her beck and call.

"Yes sweetheart?"

"Where are you taking me? What should I wear?"

"Well, you see what I have on. It's not real fancy. Business, casual."

"Okay, be out in a jiffy, thank you."

"Is that all you wanted? I think I deserve a kiss for that."

Michelle started laughing; knowing Jesse was flirting with her again. Michelle walked up to him and kissed him on the cheek.

"Mmmmmm...you sure smell good Sexy." She told him.

"Now shoo, I need to get ready." Jesse turned away with a pouty face, making Michelle laugh.

Michelle, no matter how mad she got at Jesse, he always seemed to soften her heart, making her forget about how mad he first made her. Jesse walked out of her room then and went back in the living room where George Macafey was reading through the newspaper.

"You know Jess, may I call you Jess? This old world is getting crazier every day."

"Yes, I will have to agree with you there Mr. Macafey."

Michelle continued getting ready in her bedroom, looking in her closet to decide on what to wear. She decided on wearing a pair of her favorite dark blue jeans and a flowery tan, frilly V-neck, with scalloped sleeves. Michelle changed, freshened up her makeup and re curled her hair, spraying on her perfume before she came out. When she came out, she saw that Jesse and George were engaged in conversation, so she went to find Grace Mcafee, which was in her bedroom. After a few minutes, Jesse and Michelle left to go out to eat.

"I heard you laughing when I was talking with Grace. What were you and George talking about?"

"A little bit of everything actually. He is such a card. So what did you and Grace talk about?"

"She really amazed me. Did you know that she knew that we recently found one another and that she can tell that I really love you, and have for years? Did you tell her anything?"

"Oh, really? No honey. I haven't told her anything like that. How did she know? Did you tell her?"

"No, she said the Lord told her and that she knew we were meant for each other, but we needed to put God number one in our lives, that we will have good times and some bad times ahead. But if we put all our trust in Jesus, that He'd bless our relationship."

"Huh, you don't say? George was talking along those same lines."

They arrived at a quaint little restaurant outside of the city limits that set facing a waterfall, which they took a table overlooking the beautiful view. While they were eating and enjoying one another's company as always, the waitress came and refilled their wine glasses. Soft country love songs were playing in the background. Michelle had ordered shrimp and Angel hair pasta and Jesse had ordered a juicy rib-eye steak with green beans and a side salad.

"So you were saying Jesse?"

"That I fell for you hard, years ago, and wished things could have turned out differently back then."

"Awe, really? Me too. Many times throughout my life, I'd get this weird feeling that I was being followed or watched, or someone would come into my life and I felt like they knew you. Crazy, huh?"

Jesse took a sip of his red wine, swallowing hard, watching Michelle enjoy her pasta.

"No, that's not entirely crazy."

Michelle looked at Jesse, questioning him with the tilt of her head to one side.

"Michelle, I know things about you that I wished I didn't, and other things I'm glad I do."

"Like what for instance?"

"Like I know when you...first gave into temptation."

"And how do you know that? So you're telling me that my suspicions were right all along?"

"Michelle, please don't get mad at me. I always kept an eye on you. In school and after you graduated, except for that period of time I didn't know where you moved to. You broke my heart, not telling me."

"Oh, I broke your heart huh?"

Michelle was getting mad all over again. The nerve of him keeping track of my every move, she was thinking.

"Please forgive me that I loved you a little more than I should. I couldn't bear to lose you again."

"So let me get this straight. You spied on me and followed me for years after graduation?"

"I told you I knew things about you that you wouldn't believe me."

Michelle was shaking her head in disbelief.

"Just how long have you been spying on me or keeping tabs on me Jesse? And how have you been doing it, is what I want to know."

"Michelle, I am sorry. I fell in love with you in high school and I couldn't do anything about it then. I was so afraid of losing track of you, especially when you dated Randy for two years and then off and on for eight more years."

"Oh my God Jesse. I will ask you again, just how long have you been spying on me!? You were married! And how in the Hell do you know just exactly how long I dated Randy? I figured it was a stupid little crush I had on you. After graduation, I got on with my life as best as I could. You are the one who broke my heart, You had crushed my heart so many times even though you never told me to leave you alone and stop coming around to see you or stop giving you love notes. By the way, whatever happened to all of them?"

"Would it surprise you if I told you I still have all of them?"

"Yes, but you don't do you?"

He didn't answer her but only looked into her eyes, wanting her to understand. She ate her last bite of shrimp and pasta, washing it down with a drink of wine. She looked at Jesse in dismay, still dumbfounded and angry.

"I had no idea you fell in love with me umpteen years ago. You treated everyone in class just the same."

"No, Love, I didn't. You were the only one I..."

"So what else do you know about me?"

Jesse put his head down, looking towards the waitress.

"Michelle, I am not happy or proud of the things I've done in my past. Or for the things I found out by keeping tabs on you. I am sorry and it will not happen again. I will promise you that."

"Jesse, what were you going to say when you said, I was the only, what?"

"That you were the only one I paid special attention to and had deep hidden feelings for, very strong feelings."

"Did you ever fix me up with any of your friends, secretly of course? That's what you do best, it seems is lying."

"Michelle, I never lied to you. I am not lying to you now."

"What you don't tell me IS lying, Jesse Lee Fox. So have you ever fixed me up with any of your friends, to find out information on me? Tell me!"

Michelle was looking at him, waiting for an answer, afraid she already knew the answer. Jesse was looking at her and reached for her hand but Michelle pulled it away.

"Yes, but....Michelle..."

"While we are getting everything out on the table, have you slept with Sophia?"

Jesse looked at her in shock.

"How did you know about that? Michelle, she drugged me! You have to believe me."

"Was last night the only time you slept with her?"

"Michelle"

She scooted her chair back and briskly walked out of the restaurant. She was furious with Jesse. She looked around to see where she could run to and spotted a bookstore and ran in behind a bookshelf. Jesse paid the waitress and took off looking for Michelle. He looked in the bookstore but didn't see her. Michelle was watching him as he walked out of the bookstore. She took out her cell phone and called Dawn.

"Dawn, can you come pick me up? Jesse and I got in a fight and I'm just right out of town at a bookstore next door to the café we ate at."

"I know exactly where that is. Are you okay? What happened sis?"

"He has been watching me, keeping tabs on me ever since we graduated! Can you believe it? He knows things that I have only told you! And this is the kicker. He has been fixing me up with some of his friends, getting them to go out with me!"

"That's just creepy Michelle."

"I know, right! I am so livid right now."

"Michelle, I am getting another call. Hang on."

While Michelle was waiting, she came out from hiding and looked out the window to see if she could see Jesse, but there were no signs of him.

"Michelle that was Jesse. Asked if I had heard from you?"

"How did he get your number!? What did you tell him?"

"He knew I wasn't going to tell him so he hung up."

"Are you on your way?"

"Yes, I am on my way. I will be there in about 20 minutes. Did you ask him about last night?"

"Yes, and if that was the only time he slept with her. He was shocked that I knew and asked how I knew, then said that he was drugged."

"I'm getting on the highway now sis. See you soon. Hang tough,"

"Ok, be careful Dawn. I love you sis."

"I love you too."

While Michelle was waiting on Dawn, she called Randy. She decided to take him up on his offer, to catch up on their lives. When she finished her call to Randy, Dawn pulled up and Michelle got in her car. They took off and 20 minutes later, they ended up at Dawn's house. As they were walking into Dawn's house, Dawn's phone started ringing and she answered it.

"Dawn its Jesse again. Is Michelle with you? I been calling her but it goes straight to voicemail. She must have blocked me."

"I do not want to talk to him!"

"I heard her. Please just tell her I wanted to make sure she was okay. When I couldn't find her, I was worried. Please tell her that I'm so sorry and don't even try to understand it all right now. In time, I will just have to prove to her how very much I love her. Dawn, I really do love her, in spite of what you might think of me. Is she going to stay with you tonight?"

"I, I'm not real sure, but I will tell her what you said."

Dawn told Michelle everything that Jesse told her and then Michelle asked her to take her to Randy's. Michelle was so angry with Jesse that she wanted to get back at him somehow for the things he did with Sophia in spite if he was drugged or not and for the things he knew about her from her past and how he got that information.

Dawn dropped her off at Randy's. Michelle walked up to Randy's door, knocked and waited for him to answer the door.

"Michelle, are you okay?"

"Yea, I'm fine. Let's watch that movie you suggested over the phone, shall we?"

Randy put his arm around her and led her to the sofa, and then he put the movie on.

"How about some popcorn and something to drink?"

"I will take a Dr. Pepper and popcorn sounds great. Thanks."

Randy brought her a Dr. Pepper and popped some microwave popcorn, pouring it into a bowl.

Michelle and Randy watched the movie. Throughout the evening, Randy looked at Michelle and pulled her closer with his arm around her so she could rest her head on his shoulder. Michelle was enjoying the movie and her present company, but her mind was still on Jesse. She was still furious with him. What Michelle couldn't understand is why Jesse didn't tell her how he felt about her after graduation. She knew he was married, but he could have helped her understand many things and could have prevented a lot of emotional stress throughout the years. The movie was over and Randy was caressing her neck with his fingers, making her look up at him. He bent down and kissed her.

"I've missed you Michelle. Do you think we could pick up where we left off and...?"

Michelle kissed him then and rubbed her hand on his leg, moving upwards. Randy groaned into Michele's mouth, letting her know he was enjoying her touch. Michelle knew she was doing wrong but didn't care at that particular moment.

It was the next morning and Michelle had Randy take her back to the ranch and was getting ready to get out of the car.

"Thank you Randy. I had a really nice time."

"Maybe we could do this again soon?"

He'd lean closer to give Michelle a kiss. After a short few seconds, Michelle pulled away.

"I'm sorry Randy, but I really got to think things through."

"Okay, I understand. Can I call you?"

"Sure, that will be fine. Take care Randy."

Michelle got out of his car and went inside. Grace was doing laundry and George was in the kitchen, fixing breakfast.

"Mmmmmm sure smells really good Mr. Macafey."

"Hi Michelle. I didn't hear you come in. Would you like to join us? Eggs, bacon, pancakes, orange juice and coffee."

"Yes, that sounds delicious. Thank you."

"Hi Michelle. I didn't hear you come in. Is everything alright?"

Grace asked, looking at her. Michelle was silent and almost in tears, but just shook her head. They sat the food on the table and Grace put the plates, silverware and glasses on the table.

After breakfast, Michelle helped Grace clean up the kitchen and began to open up to her.

"Grace, Jesse and I had a fight last night. He made me so angry that I just wanted to get back at him."

"Jesse came by last night and told us everything."

"He did? What did he say?"

"Yes. He really loves you Michelle. He has for quite a long time."

"Yea, I know. That's what he claims. What I don't understand is why couldn't he have told me this years ago, after graduation? And why on earth did he fix me up with his friends!"

Tears started strolling down her cheeks as Grace hugged her.

"Michelle, all I know is what God revealed to me and what Jesse told me. Everything happens for a reason and in God's perfect timing."

After Michelle stopped crying, Grace gave her a couple tissues and Michelle went to her room, sat down at her laptop computer and opened it. She saw her editor had sent her an email. It read:

Hi Michelle,

I have some good news and some bad news. The bad news is that you have to fly out to L.A. This week, preferably as soon as possible. Let me know when you read this. And the good news is that after all the rewrites and editing you have done on your second novel, it is finally getting published. But wait, there is more. The publisher who is publishing it is very interested in turning it into a big time movie. Ok be sure and call me ASAP after you read this.

Waiting to hear from you.

Patty Black

Michelle looked at the time and date of when she had sent the email and it was just last night at 7:27 p.m. It was Sunday morning now at almost eleven. Michelle was so excited she had to call her mom.

"Mom! Guess what? Patty my editor emailed me and told me my second book is going to get published finally! And that they were interested in turning it into a big time movie production! I can't believe it mom! I am so excited! You are the first person I've told."

"Oh honey, I am so proud of you. I knew you could do it. Congratulations honey. You did it. All that determination paid off, didn't?"

"Yes, yes it did! Thank you for all your encouragement. I love you mom. I wanted you to be the first person to know. Please tell dad and everyone. Oh and I have to take the next flight to L.A. too. I've got to call Patty. I'll call you when I get back from L, A.mom. I love you and thank you so much for being behind me in my writing career! Talk to you soon. Bye"

Michelle couldn't hold it back any longer and shouted out loud.

THANK YOU PRECIOUS JESUS FOR LETTING MY BOOK GET PUBLISHED! THANK YOU SO VERY MUCH I LOVE YOU YOU DID IT ALL AND I GIVE YOU ALL THE PRAISE, GLORY AND HONOR YOU ARE SO RIGHTLY DESERVE GLORY BE TO GOD IN THE MOST HIGH

Happy tears fell from her eyes this time as she lifted her hands to Praise God. She was praying silently when Grace came in to congratulate her. When Grace left her room, Michelle called Patty her editor, and then packed her bags to catch the next flight to L.A. She arrived at LAX that evening and met with Patty as she picked her up from the airport. They left the airport and went to a nice restaurant to get a bite to eat while they discussed the details of Michelle's book getting published and made into a movie. After their dinner meeting, Patty offered Michelle to stay with her at her apartment and Michelle took her up on her offer. The next morning, Patty drove her back to the airport.

When Michelle arrived back home the next day, Grace and George had left a note for her, telling her they had to cut their stay short that some emergency came up and had to leave early. As she was reading the note, the telephone rang.

"Hello?"

"Hi Love. Where have you been? I sure have missed you. I'm sorry about the other night. Will you ever forgive me, please?"

Dawn was calling her cell phone as Michelle looked to see who it was.

"Jesse, I'm sorry, but I'll call you, Dawn is calling."

"May I come over? Will you let me do that?"

"I don't know. I've got to answer the phone. Bye"

Michelle answered her cell phone.

"Hey sis! Where have you been? I've been worried about you!"

"I'm fine. I flew to L.A. to meet with Patty my editor. My second book is being published and made into a movie! I am so excited Dawn!"

"Wow! That's awesome sis! Congratulations! We need to celebrate!"

"Yes, we do!"

"Ugh, but first, I have to tell you something. Michelle, Jesse caught Dr. Viza, Michael and I kissing in his office the other day. That's what I needed to tell you. Yes, I was trying to fix you up with Michael, when you had your accident. I am so sorry. So when Jesse caught Michael and me kissing at the hospital, Jesse came up to us. Oh my gosh Michelle, are you still there?"

"Yes. He is on his way over here probably, so please hurry and tell me already."

"Michelle, Mr. Jesse Fox gave Michael a left hook and started giving us the third degree about being faithful, betraying friends and all. Oh he was furious. I never saw him THAT mad, since that one time in class. He proceeded to tell me how rotten it was to be betraying my husband like that and my best friend. I guess you told him you thought I was fixing you up with Michael. Then he was telling Michael if he had ANY intentions with his granddaughter Barbie, that he best think twice before he even considers it. That if he even as much as looked at her crossed eyed, that he hoped his eyes stuck like that. And that if he ever hurt her in anyway, he wouldn't live to tell about it."

Michelle was laughing so hard, she had tears in her eyes.

"Well, I'm glad you are taking it well."

"I'm sorry Dawn. I could see Jesse taking up for his granddaughter. He worships her. I was remembering when he got so mad in class and threatened to flunk every one of us if no one confessed of stealing the nine weeks test with answers, out of his briefcase and giving them out. Ok, so, how do you know Michael again?"

"He is Jake's best friend. They grew up together. But he had moved away their junior year and had been gone until now. He recently moved back here and is staying at our house until he finds his own place to live. I have always thought he was cute. Do you remember that weekend before Jake and I got married?"

"Yea, I think so. You told me your parents wanted to spend some time with you as a family one last time before you got married. And that you went up to the family cabin over the weekend, but it wasn't with your parents. It was with...Michael! Oh Dawn! I can't believe this. Are you and Michael having another affair?"

"No! The kiss just happened, like for old times' sake I guess. I don't know. But I don't believe it will ever happen again. God, it was like I was back in his class again!"

Michelle started laughing again, motioning Jesse to come in.

"Sis, he just walked in. I have to go, but hang in there. I will call you later."

"Michelle, wait. Will you forgive me?"

"For what? There is nothing to forgive you for. I love you. I always will."

Jesse came up behind her, wrapping his arms around her waist, kissing her on the neck.

"One more question. What happened the other night with Randy?"

"Ugh, later sis...goodbye."

Michelle ended the call,

"Hi handsome. Where have you been all my life?"

Michelle turned around to face him, giving him a quick kiss on the cheek.

"Well hello Babe. Is that all I get?"

Jesse tried to pull her closer to him but Michelle pulled away. Jesse was looking intently at her.

"I see you are still upset about the other night. Who's Randy, as if I don't know already?"

"I was afraid you heard Dawn. He is just a friend Jesse. He wanted to catch up on the past and shoot the breeze. So, where have you been all this time Jesse? I want to know. Out with your neighbor Sophia perhaps?"

"Oh, just a friend, huh? A boyfriend from the past perhaps? Is that why you didn't come home that night, trying to rekindle an old flame?"

Michelle shook her head in dismay, looking down to the floor. When Michelle looked back up at Jesse, he was still looking at her.

"Did you call him after our fight the other night? Or did he just happen to call you?"

"Jesse, stop it! Dawn ran into him the other day and he was asking about me and she gave him my number. Honestly, I believe she had him call me to get me distracted away from you, to tell you the truth."

"Oh Dawn! That figures! Yea, let's talk about her. I'm sure she told you about me finding her and that so called quack of a Dr. kissing in his office. I didn't know you were like her, going behind my back and betraying me like that. I guess it's true. Best friends do stick together like glue."

"Jesse, stop putting Dawn down like that! She is like my sister and I consider her family. About Randy, I told you he was just a friend. Besides, I do NOT need your permission to go out with my friends. I will NOT be controlled like that!"

"Oh yes, you most certainly do young lady, if your so called "friends", so happened to be guys! And especially ex-boyfriend, nonetheless!"

Michelle went to the kitchen, not answering him, pouring herself a glass of red wine. Jesse followed after her.

"What, is he younger than me? Better looking? Richer? What?"

"Jesse! If I knew I was going to be interrogated when you came over, I wouldn't have let you in. I don't need this! And it's about time you answer my questions!"

"Well, I never in a million years thought that you'd be like Dawn. Going behind my back and betray me like that! That hurts."

"Oh, don't you even preach to me about betrayal, after what I saw you and Sophia doing the other night!"

"What did you see exactly and how?"

Michelle didn't answer him.

"Jesse, for the last time, I didn't betray you. Besides, I didn't hear from you for a few days. I had no idea where you were, if you ran off with what's her name, your neighbor and got married or what. You STILL, haven't told me ANYTHING really! And that hurts."

Michelle took a drink of her glass of red wine and then Jesse took her glass and took a drink, then pulled her into his arms and kissed her passionately and then looked deep into her eyes.

"Michelle, I am sorry. I have no right to accuse you or treat you like I just did. Will you ever forgive me, please? I love you. I have for a very long time. And I hope you love me too and feel the same way about me as I feel about you. I don't want to ever lose you. And no, I haven't been out with my neighbor, Sophia. I have been working on a project of my own, that requires me to go out of town occasionally. I don't want to tell you because it's a surprise for you. Now, will you please forgive me? I'd much rather make love and not war."

Jesse reached for her glass again, but Michelle pulled it away from him. He was looking into her eyes, searching her soul.

"Michelle, can you please forgive me for being so in love with you, that I want you all to myself?"

"That depends."

"On what Love?"

He tries again for her wine glass, stepping closer, but she continued to pull it away. Michelle was leaning up against the kitchen counter now, as Jesse's voice was softer and not as aggressive. She could smell his clean fresh scent and heavenly cologne, which intoxicated her with desire.

"If you don't EVER, interrogate me like that again, EVER! Or give Sophia the time of day ever again. And lock your freaking doors when your home!"

Michelle held his stare, looking into his beautiful, deep dark brown eyes, taking in his wonderful scent and wanting desperately to kiss him.

"Well, only if you don't give me ANY reason to NOT give you a reason to interrogate you like that and I wou..."

Jesse stopped mid-sentence and grabbed her glass and took a drink, then suddenly kissed her passionately, pulling her next to him.

"Mmmmmm..."

Jesse pulled away, looking into Michelle's mysterious cat eyes.

"Is that a good enough reason to forgive me?"

"Ugh, I need a lot more convincing than that."

Jesse took her by her soft hand and led her out of the kitchen and into the living room onto the sofa.

"A lot more convincing, huh? You drive a hard bargain Michelle Renee' Mertz."

"Yep, and don't you ever forget it either."

Jesse began kissing her as he rubbed her shoulders softly, caressing them. Then he slowly started kissing her neck, working his way down to the top of her button on her shirt. She'd be enjoying his touch and be running her fingers through his soft pretty brown hair.

"Mmmmmm, Jess"

"Hmm my baby love. Are you convinced yet?"

"Not even close, but it will have to do for now, I guess. You could try and convince me all night long, but still yet, you haven't even scratched the surface."

"Oh, I beg to differ with you there sweetheart."

He slowly caressed her bare legs, moving closer to her thigh, letting his fingertips tease and caress. They engaged in another passionate kiss, as Michelle reached out to him. Jesse pulled away as he reached her hand before it reached its destination.

"Oh my baby love, as much as I want you, we best stop right now. I'm sorry I let it get this far. And I am so sorry for how I treated you tonight, and everything. Will you ever accept my apologies?"

"Well, you do some pretty heavy convincing."

Jesse laughed out loud giving her a hug.

"So, are we ok? Is all minds clear?"

"Not so fast. So where were you all that time Jesse?"

"Darlin, I told you. I had a business trip to take. I am working on something that requires me to be out of pocket occasionally, but I believe it's all taken care of now and I can spend more time with you. Unless you want to spend your time with Randy."

"Jesse Lee Fox! I am warning you."

He laughed out loud again and she hit him on his arm.

"Ouch. Well, I hope that you want to spend more time with me than with him."

"Just don't make me mad anymore and I will always want to spend time with you."

"Oh, is that how it is, huh? Only if I don't make you mad?"

Jesse was teasing her, caressing her leg again.

"Yes".

"If we don't have fights, we can't kiss and make up, now can we?"

He smiled at her, winked and kissed her again, but Michelle pulled away quickly.

"OMG! I almost forgot to tell you! Look what you do to me Jesse! I can't believe I haven't told you yet."

Jesse raised his eyebrows, questioning her with a smile.

"Well, let's hear it."

"My second book is finally getting published! And possibly made into a movie! Jesse, I did it! Well, God did it! I give Him all the glory, honor and praise for it, but I am so excited!"

"That's my girl! I told you that you would do it. That is great Michelle! That is really wonderful! I am so very proud of you!"

Jesse hugged her tightly. After a few moments, they would pull away. Jesse left and Michelle got ready for bed. But before she laid her head down to rest, she opened her Bible up to the book of Romans, chapter 8. She read:

> *There is therefore now no condemnation to them which are in Christ Jesus, who walks not after the flesh, but after the Spirit.* Michelle read all of chapter 8 in Romans, and then asked forgiveness for letting her flesh rule over her with Randy, and then she fell fast asleep.

Chapter Nine

The next morning, after Michelle finished her chores outside, feeding the horses and cleaning the barn, she went back up to the house to return phone calls she had missed while she was outside. She called her parents first.

"Hey dad, what's going on...?" "Oh nothing much. Where have you been? We have been worried about you. Mom has been trying to call you."

"I'm sorry I didn't call you guys. I have been outside cleaning the barn and feeding Abraham and Sarah. Did mom tell you my second book is getting published and possibly into a movie?"

"Yea she did! We are so proud of you Michelle. You betcha we are!"

"Thanks dad! I am so excited!" I thank God and give Him all the glory, honor and praise, because He is the One Who did it, not me."

"Well you had to write it. You deserve credit too."

"Yea, but if it wasn't for God Who inspired me and gave me the desire to write and minister to people in this way, then it wouldn't have been written or published. I truly believe that. I remember before I started writing this book, I asked God to help me in writing it and to help me get it published and made into a movie. And God always hears and answers our prayers, one way or another."

"Here is mom. Do you want to yak at her a minute?"

"Sure dad. I love you. See you guys soon."

"I love you too, you betcha." Michelle laughed.

Her dad recently started saying that and it always made her laugh. She talked to her mom a few minutes then she called Dawn.

"Hey Dork."

"What have you been up to?"

"Oh I just been cleaning the barn and feeding the horses. What have you been doing?"

"Forget about that. You need to tell me what happened with you and Randy the other night."

"Oh we just watched a movie."

"And...Michelle, I know there is more to the story than that. Did you guys kiss?" Michelle started laughing.

"You had sex with him, didn't you? Dawn started laughing.

"Dawn, I shouldn't have gone to his house. I feel so ashamed."

"Don't feel bad. It happens to the best of us."

"Yea, but I shouldn't have led him on. I noticed he has called me about three times now since the other night. I have been avoiding him."

"Well, so, what now? Did you and Jesse make up?"

"Yes, we made up. He's still real secretive though, which makes me keep my guard up."

"Yes, by all means keep your guard up. I believe Jesse is on the warpath, and ready to pounce on someone. I still can't believe how he reacted the other day between me and Michael."

"Yea, he mentioned that last night, accusing me of betraying him and being just like you."

"Oh did he now? That...! Did you ask him about his night with Sophia? Did you show him the video?"

"Dawn, sis, I took up for you. I told him that I loved you like family and that he shouldn't talk about you that way. Calm down!"

"Well thank you. It still makes me mad at him."

"I know. It does me too but will you promise me something, please? Jesse says he loves me. And if we double date, I want you to treat him with utmost respect, okay?" "Oh alright sis. I will do it for you. I promise I will be on my best behavior around you two and be nice to the old Codger."

"Okay, thank you sis. It really means a lot to me. I promise I will keep my guard up and be careful."

"Oh hey, I noticed Jake mowed while I was gone. Tell him thank you."

"Jake hasn't mowed out there for a few days."

"Hmm, maybe Jesse did."

"Maybe Randy did? Well, if for some reason Jesse and you don't work out; sounds like Randy be willing to take you back."

"I didn't make him any promises. I can't believe Jesse reacted like that with you two kissing."

"I know, right! You should have seen him. I'm serious. He was scaring me sis. It was just like being back in his class again. Remember how I could push his buttons and make him mad." Dawn laughed.

"He told me that I better think twice on what I just did, kissing Michael, and that if I loved my husband at all, that I better concentrate on him, and work towards making that love grow, like it was in the beginning."

"He must remember how you and Jake were always hanging all over each other in high school and at the football games."

"Yea, that must have been it. I just remembered that it was Mr. Fox, who caught Jake and me making out at the top of the bleachers in the gym during one of the Homecoming football games. Everyone was outside, so we thought we were alone. Jake and I were getting it on, hot and heavy, when Mr. Fox turned on a bright flashlight, shining it into our faces."

Michelle started laughing.

"I remember you telling me about that. That's when your bra broke, isn't it? And he gave you both detention for a week, but not at the same time."

"Yea and we had to write an essay on how wild animals mate in the wild, because that's what we were acting like."

They both laughed. "Then the following week, he picked me to read aloud everyday starting off with the essay I wrote!"

"I remember that too! Oh my, what punishment. I wonder if Jake remembers all that."

"I don't know. I'll have to ask him"

"Maybe you ought to remind him. I want to repay you guys for all the hard work you did around here while my ankle was healing. I want to keep the kids for a weekend, so you and Jake can rekindle that old flame again."

"Oh sis, you don't have to do that. I believe I learned my lesson. Mr. Fox really opened my eyes."

"I bet it's awkward with Michael staying with you still, isn't he?"

"No, he moved to a hotel that same night."

"What did he tell Jake?"

"That since he got his first check from working at the hospital, he wanted to move out. Jake doesn't know about what happened or before we got married."

"I hear you loud and clear sis. You know I will not say anything to him."

"Oh I know that."

"And what did Jesse say to Michael again?"

"He told him if he was flirting with his granddaughter that he best stop messing around with a married woman such as me. And that if he heard anything that Michael was doing to upset his granddaughter Barbie, that he had to answer to him again and that it wouldn't be pretty at all." Michelle started laughing again.

"He's always been protective of his precious granddaughter, since she's the only one he has."

"No doubt about that!"

"Well, I better get out of here before Jesse gets here. Oh never mind, here he is coming up the walkway. I will talk to you later sis."

They hung up the phone and Michelle went to the door to greet him with a kiss.

"Hi handsome. What brings you by?"

"Oh a lovely lady, by the name of Michelle. Is everything okay?"

"Yea, why? Hey thanks for mowing my grass Jess. That was very nice of you."

"I didn't mow your grass love. Maybe your boyfriend did. You know the one you went out with the night of our argument."

Michelle just shook her head in dismay, and walked to the kitchen to get her a glass of ice tea.

"I thought we had hashed all this out last night Jesse?"

"That was before your grass got mowed by your, ugh so called ex-boyfriend."

"Oh good grief, here we go again. Jesse, look, go home. I can't deal with you when you are like this."

Jesse didn't move and wanted to argue again.

"Jesse, if you don't leave, I am going to call the police. Now get out!"

Michelle pointed to the door and Jesse reluctantly left.

Chapter Ten

The next morning, Michelle woke up to her cell phone ringing. It was Jesse. "Good morning. Did you sleep well?"

"Well enough I reckon. Did you?"

"Not as good as I'm sure I would have, sleeping next to you. Are you still mad at me?"

"Awe, that's sweet. It's still early."

"Yes, it is my Love. It's 7:30 a,m., to be exact. If you don't have any prior engagements today, why don't I come over and pick you up and we go out and celebrate the whole day that your second book getting published. And to make up to you for my jealous tendencies."

"That sounds like a plan. Where are we going?"

"Well, we will start out by going to eat breakfast."

"Mmmmmm...sounds great. Eggs, sunny side up, as long as the white part is fully cooked, crispy bacon, fried, crispy hash browns and maybe some corn beef hash and OJ."

"That's a tall order, but I know just the place that can fill it. I will see you in a little while."

"Ok, I will be ready."

They ended their call as Michelle got out of bed and went to the restroom, walked to the front door to unlock it for Jesse and then went to take a shower. When Michelle stood up from blow drying her hair, Jesse was standing in her doorway watching her and she jumped and screamed.

"I didn't hear you come in. You scared me."

"Obviously. I'm sorry babe. I didn't mean to scare you. I was enjoying watching you."

"I will forgive you this once, but don't ever let it happen again". Michelle teased.

He embraces her with a loving kiss.

"Mmmmmm....you smell so divine and taste oh so delicious baby."

Jesse started kissing her neck and moved his roaming hands to bring her closer to him.

"Ugh...Darlin...."

"It's getting really difficult to keep my hands away from your beautiful body, my love."

They kissed passionately and Michelle's hands roamed too, reaching her destination this time, and rubbed him there.

"Awe....*mmm*...Michelle...."

"Hmmm...?"

Jesse pulled away slowly; cupping her towel covered breasts, but quickly moved them around her back and pulled her into him to kiss her again. He walked her backwards until they fell onto her bed.

"Michelle, please stop me if you don't want this to go any further." Jesse looked into her eyes with passion, searching for her answer, as he caressed her bare thigh, just below her tan shorts she had on. Michelle kissed him again, not saying a word, reaching for him. Couple hours later, when Michelle rolled over, she looked at Jesse sound asleep beside her with his arm around her. She looked at the clock and it was 11:37 a.m. She reached for her cell phone and checked to see if she had any missed calls. As she was looking, her phone rang. She slipped out of bed and went into the living room to answer it.

"Hello?"

"Hello Michelle. It's Randy. How have you been? I've called you a few times and left you messages. Are you okay?"

Michelle then walked to the kitchen as to keep from waking Jesse. She really didn't need him listening and finding out who she was talking to.

"Michelle? Are you there?"

"Yes, yes I'm here Randy. Uhg, this really isn't a good time right now. I'm fine. I'm sorry I haven't returned your calls. I've been so busy since the last time I saw you. I went to L.A., to get my second novel published."

"Oh that's great Babe! Congratulations! We need to celebrate!"

"I will give you a signed copy of it when it comes out."

Michelle saw Jesse getting up.

"Randy, I really have to run. I'm sorry. Hey, did you mow my grass the other day?"

"Yes, it was me. I came over to check on you and noticed you were gone. And then noticed the grass was getting high and the mower was right there. I hope you didn't mind?"

"No, not at all. I appreciated it. Thank you!"

Jesse walked up behind her and kissed her neck, trying to eavesdrop on who Michelle was talking to.

"Okay, you are welcome Michelle. Call me sometime, anytime, okay?" Randy pleaded.

"I have to go now. Bye."

And Michelle ended the call. Michelle turned around to face Jesse and kissed him lovingly.

"Hi my sexy, good looking, handsome Fox. Did you sleep well?"

"Like a baby. Better than ever, since I was next to the love of my life. Did you?"

"Very well."

"Who was on the phone?"

Michelle knew he was going to ask and was dreading to tell him, fearing his response.

"Uhg, your least favorite person."

"Did you find out who mowed the grass for you?"

"Yes."

"That was him on the phone, wasn't it?"

"Jesse, please. Let's not get into this conversation again. I certainly don't want to fight with you."

"Oh, but it's so much fun making out, I mean making up." Michelle started laughing. They got ready and left to go eat breakfast at a nice little café and then went to Dollywood. They walked, talked, laughed, rode rides and saw different shows, all day long. It was getting late into the evening and so they left. Jesse took her home and promised he'd be back over the next day.

The next few weeks went by as Jesse and Michelle spent quality time together enjoying each other's company, getting to know one another. It was early morning when Jesse came over to help Michelle feed the horses, clean the barn, mow and weed eat. When they finally finished everything, it was 12:30 in the afternoon.

"Man, I'm beat. This is hard for an old man."

"Oh Jesse, you are not old. You are as young as you feel."

"Well, at the moment, my body is telling me I feel ancient. I think I need a good ole shower, a nice meal, and then a nap."

"Oh, do you now?"

"Yes ma'am. Do you mind if I use your shower and get cleaned up? I promise I will be on my best behavior."

"No, of course not. Did you bring a change of clothes?"

"As a matter of fact, I did. They are in the car."

"Ok, why don't I go get them while you start your shower? You can find everything you need in the bathroom closet."

"Ok Love, thank you. Ugh, I may need your help scrubbing my back."

Michelle grinned at him.

"I'll be busy fixing us a nice meal, as you put it, after I bring in your clothes, Darlin. Guess you are on your own."

"You can't blame a guy for trying."

While Jesse was taking a shower, Michelle prepared a fresh salad and made up 2 grilled cheese sandwiches with fried bologna. After they ate lunch, Jesse lay on her bed and rested while she took a shower and cleaned up. When Michelle finished in the bathroom, she found Jesse sound asleep. She lay down beside him quietly, being careful not to wake him. Michelle laid on her stomach facing Jesse and watched him sleep until she closed her eyes and fell asleep too. It wasn't until a little after 4 p.m. when Michelle woke up to Jesse rubbing her back.

"Hello sleeping beauty." Michelle smiled.

"How long have you been awake?"

"Not long. I was enjoying watching you sleep peacefully. We had ourselves a couple hour nap."

Jesse kissed her lips, looking at her. He kissed her again more passionately.

"You are so beautiful Michelle and it is getting very difficult being close to you like this and not be tempted to lavish you like a wild beast."

"I feel the same way about you Jess. What are we going to do about that?" Michelle reluctantly got up and went into the bathroom, looking at herself in the mirror, and then started brushing her tangled hair. It was still a little damp from her shower earlier. Jesse came up behind her putting his hands around her, looking at her in the mirror.

"We look pretty good together, don't we Love?"

"Not too shabby. You make me look and feel like Ms. America."

"And you, my precious Love of my life, make me look and feel like Captain America."

Michelle started laughing as he'd be kissing her neck until his cell phone started ringing.

Jesse grunted as he stopped kissing her and answered his phone.

"Hello? Yes. Really? Ok, I will..."

Jesse walked out of the bathroom then as if to keep Michelle from hearing. Michelle used the restroom, touched up her makeup and went into the living room where Jesse was still talking on the phone. She was watching him, listening to him until he was finished with his conversation.

"Who was that, Captain America?" Jesse laughed.

"Oh, it was a business associate, and then my daughter beeped in."

"Is everything okay?"

"Yes, everything is okay. It is nothing to worry your pretty little self about."

"Ok, if you say so."

"Michelle, I love you."

Michelle was silent for a moment. That was the first time he actually said the words to her like that. He said he loves me.

"I love you too Jesse."

Michelle smiled at him, but got the impression he was holding something back from telling her something but didn't have a clue on what it could be. They decided to go to the mall and look around. As they were strolling hand in hand, Jesse stopped in front of a jewelry store window, looking at the engagement rings they had displayed.

"Which one do you like?" he asked Michelle, looking at her. With wide eyes, she smiled looking at him, and then to the rings in the window.

"Mmmmmm, honestly, I'm not too crazy about any of them. They are way too expensive."

"I'm not concerned with the prices right now. I just want to see what your tastes and likes are."

"Why?" Michelle was testing him but he didn't answer her.

"Let's go inside and look around."

Jesse coaxed her in and they began to look at some rings. Jesse wanted to know what size Michelle's ring finger was so he picked out a ring for her to try on. The Jeweler took the ring out and proceeded to tell them about the ring.

"Beautiful, isn't? I believe it's a size 7, but let's check to make sure." He took it and slid it on the ring sizer.

"Yes, it is a size 7 and it looks like that is a perfect fit for you."

Michelle slipped the ring on and looked at it. and It did fit perfectly.

"It is very pretty, but it's just not me Jesse."

Michelle slipped the ring off and handed it back to the Jeweler.

"Thank you."

"Thank you for stopping by."

They walked out of the jewelry store and stopped to watch the puppies in the pet store window. There were four different breeds which included a St. Bernard, a Basset Hound, a Shi-Tzu and a Yorkshire terrier.

"Oh my goodness. Are these not the cutest puppies you have ever seen? Just look at them Jess. Awe..."

"Which one is your favorite?"

"Are you kidding? I love them all!"

Michelle exclaimed and walked in and around to where the puppies were. Jesse was watching her play with them all and noticed she kept playing with the St. Bernard the most, which gave him an idea.

"You didn't like the rings we were looking at but you fall head over heels with these critters."

"What can I say? Diamonds are a girl's best friend, but so are dogs and I'd rather have a four-legged best friend."

"Oh I'm sure Dawn wouldn't like that." Jesse retorted.

"Jesse, stop it. Be nice. Dawn would tell you the same thing."

They left the pet store and continued walking the rest of the Mall. As they were getting into Jesse's car, Michelle asked him two questions.

"So, what size ring do you wear Jess?"

"I'm not entirely sure my Love. This ring I have on here is a size 9 1/2 If I remember correctly."

"And which puppy did you like the best Jesse?"

"I think the little tri-color Shi-Tzu took a liking to me for some reasons."

Jesse took Michelle home after they stopped and ate at their favorite Chinese buffet. Michelle hadn't said two words to him after he told her he was leaving again in the morning and wouldn't tell her where he was going. Madison, who normally worked the cashier counter came and refilled their wine glasses.

"May I get you anything else you two love birds?"

"Ugh, I'm not feeling the love too much right now Madison. I just told her I was leaving again in the morning."

"Don't forget to tell her that you didn't tell me just where you're leaving to or with whom! You and Sofia are probably leaving together having one last fling or something."

"Michelle Love, I didn't mean to upset you. That wasn't my intentions at all Babe. ``I love you."

"Michelle, I know Mr. Fox wouldn't be unfaithful to you. And as for not telling you where he's going, I grant you it's not what you think."

"Ok Madison, thank you dear. That will be all."

Jesse told Madison. Jesse took Michelle home as Michelle went inside the ranch house, which was still for sale. Michelle closed and locked the door behind her, leaving Jesse standing there on the front porch, without saying bye to him.

Chapter Eleven

A few days went by without hearing from Jesse and Michelle started to worry so she drove over to Jesse's house, hoping that his granddaughter would be there. When she drove into his driveway, Michelle saw his granddaughter's car, and then she saw Jesse's car parked next door at his neighbor Sophia's driveway. This really infuriated Michelle and stormed over to her house and knocked on her front door. There was no answer, so she knocked on the door again, and rang her doorbell repeatedly. Michelle waited but still, no one answered the door. Michelle walked over to Jesse's and knocked on his front door. The window screen was open so she hollered at Barbie. A couple minutes later and Barbie came to the door.

"Oh hi Michelle. How are you? Come on in. I just got off the phone with grampa."

"Hmm, how is the ole coot? Barbie, I get so mad at him for not telling me where he goes, "out of pocket", as he puts it."

"I'm sorry for my grandpa being difficult sometimes. He told me y'all had a fight before he left. I told him he shouldn't be so difficult. He didn't appreciate that too much. But I also told him to just leave you alone and let you cool off instead of trying to make up with you right away."

"Is that why I hadn't heard from him? And why is his car parked next door?" Barbie started laughing.

"I'm sorry Michelle, but grandpa knew you'd be asking about that, and he told me to tell you and I quote, "No, I am not with my neighbor and that she asked to borrow it while I am away on business since her car is in the shop." Michelle laughed out loud.

"Oh Jesse, he knows me quite well. Your grandpa, what am I going to do with him?"

"I'm sorry Michelle. He made me promise not to tell you where he was or what he's doing. He swore me to secrecy, but I can vouch for him that he has been working on a project for quite some time now. I believe he has accomplished it and just wants to tell you in person and surprise you."

"He does enjoy surprising me alright. I told him I'm not a kid anymore that I don't need surprises all the time, but of course, he still does it."

"That's my gramps for ya. He still brings me back surprises too, whenever he leaves on his trips."

"So when is he coming home? It's been a week, but feels like forever. I just wanted to make sure he was okay."

"Yes, he's just fine. He told me he was on his way home now and should be back in the early morning hours. In fact, I have to pick him up at the airport. He is going to call me when he arrives."

"Ok Barbie, thank you. You're pretty smart. Or I should say, pretty and smart."

"Oh Michelle, that's what he tells me. Thank you. I just wished I could find someone as good as my gramps. Oh, by the way, Michael, Dr. Viza, turned out to be a real jerk. I turned him down flat, when I heard about what happened with your friend."

"Good for you Barb! Yea sounds like he's a real piece of work alright."

"You and grandpa seem to be a perfect match made in Heaven, although he's difficult at times. I hadn't seen him this happy in a long time. I wanted to let you know that."

"Thank you, Barbie. That means a lot to hear you say that. I know I really love him. I have for a long time since high school. I remember when you were born. He was so happy that day in class but wished he could have been there. He is so very proud of you Barbie."

"I know. He tells me that often. He's pretty special in my life. He and grams have always been there for me."

"Yea, apparently he's been there for me too, just without me knowing it!" Barbie laughed.

"I know. I don't know how he does it. There have been times he'd bring up things I had said or done that I didn't know he knew about. But he knew it somehow. As long as you two known one another and you keep treating him nice and take good care of him, you and I will get along just great. But I'm sure you will. There is no doubt in my mind that you won't. As for gramps, I don't believe he would ever mistreat you in any way, shape or form. But if he ever starts getting too suspicious of your love for him or whatever, then I will reassure him. I believe you and I will be seeing a lot of each other."

"Thank you again Barbie."

"Anytime Michelle. I have the next 4 days off after working two weeks, nonstop practically. I have a date tonight with this new intern. He's so cute, pretty smile with dimples. He's nothing like Dr. Viza."

"Well, just be careful. You can't trust hardly anyone these days. You call me if you need to, okay?"

"That's exactly what grandpa said! Okay, I will. You two really are meant for each other. You guys think a lot alike."

When Michelle was going to her car, she saw Sophia in her front yard watering her garden and went over there. She didn't know exactly what she was going to say, but she knew she had to set some things straight.

"Hey, Sophia. I don't know what you intend with Jesse, but he's mine now. Stay away from him! And if you don't..."

"And if I don't what? What are you going to do about it?"

"Just stay away from him. Avoid him like the plague."

"Or what? I want to know."

Michelle reached up and slapped her face and then took her water hose from her, pushing her down and sprayed her with the water hose before she turned and walked back to her car. Before she got into her car, she noticed Sophia was still on the ground in shock.

"That! That will happen again if you don't stay away from my Jesse. He's mine, got it!" Sophia got up then, rubbing her face and then shaking her fists at Michelle as she drove off.

"You will pay for this!"

Michelle went back home after leaving Jesse's house. She was glad he was alright, but sure wondered where he could be. She felt satisfied she cleared up any misunderstandings Sophia had about stealing Jesse from her. She kept busy that evening by doing chores around the house and taking care of the horses, giving them fresh water and hay. When she went back up to the house, she had a missed call from Jesse.

"Michelle honey, I'll see you in the morning. I sure have missed you my Love. I am looking forward to seeing you again. I have a surprise for you, well two really. See you soon. I love you. I really do love you."

Of course it was her Jesse. She was so happy to hear his incredible sexy voice again. She took a shower and got comfortable. She watched her favorite TV preacher, Dr. Charles and then read in her Bible awhile before she drifted off into a deep sleep. She started dreaming as different scenes flashed by.

The first scene was in Heaven, where she was sitting on a blanket under a huge Oak tree, having a picnic with Jesus. She had on a garment that was all white and looked like a bed sheet. Jesus was wearing the same thing. They were talking about all the things Michelle didn't understand in her life. Then the scene changed to a big beautiful house. She saw laughing children playing, running around trying to catch pretty butterflies. There were all kinds of people there, all nationalities, short, tall, skinny and fat. Michelle saw the cutest little blonde puppy that came up to her wagging its tail.

Michelle woke up laughing and then looked at the clock to see it was 2:45 a.m. Michelle got up and went to use the restroom, and took a drink of her melted down iced tea that she had from earlier on her night stand. She fell back asleep and continued to dream. But this time it wasn't Heaven. It was a very dark, very hot place which represented Hell. There was blood curdling screams coming from a big black hole in the middle of this ugly, scary place. When she proceeded to look down the black hole, she could see a fire burning below with people standing around, shielding themselves from demons tormenting them, poking at them, making fun of them, and pushing them into the fiery pit. Others would be chained up by their ankles on their hands and knees, looking up and calling out to Jesus and their loved ones to save them. Michelle kept hearing the people's cry for help. "HELP ME! PLEASE SAVE ME JESUS! PLEASE! I SORRY...SO SORRY! NO! NO! GET AWAY FROM ME! NO!" The demons would be grabbing at the ones crying out, one by one and throwing them into the eternal pit of Hell Fire. This dream, like the other she had, were so real and so vivid that she woke up again, crying. She couldn't get those anguished cries for help out of her head.

Michelle turned her bedside lamp on and reached for her Bible. She turned to the book of Revelation 3:3-6. It read:

> 3) Remember therefore how thou hast received and heard, and hold fast, and repent, turn away from. If therefore thou shalt not watch, I will come in as a thief, and thou shalt not know what hour I will come upon thee. 4) Thou has a few names even in Sardis which have not defiled their garments; and they shall walk with me in white: for they are worthy. 5) He that overcometh, the same shall be clothed in white raiment; and I will not blot out his name out of the Book of Life. But I will confess his name before my Father, and before his angels. 6) He that hath an ear, let him hear what the Spirit saith unto the churches.

Michelle started to pray.

> "Oh dear Heavenly Father God, in Jesus name, please help me to be more like You, and to be a witness to others. I know I fail You a lot. I do want to be used by You and to testify what a Mighty Powerful, Loving God You are. Please forgive me of all my sins and cleanse me from ALL unrighteousness."

Michelle continued praying silently for a while and then turned off her light, rolling over to try and fall asleep again. When morning came and the sun was shining into her bedroom, she woke up to a scratching sound. She got up to investigate. She looked out her window but couldn't see anything. She went into the living room and heard a whimpering sound, and then more scratching. As she came closer to the front door, it was louder and she opened it to find a little St. Bernard puppy. Michelle looked around but didn't see anyone that it could belong to. She opened up the screen door, bent down and picked up the puppy. There was a little brown barrel around its neck with a note that said open and read note first. Michelle looked around again and was sure to find Jesse somewhere, but he was nowhere to be found. She opened the little brown barrel, finding another note with a red velvet heart shaped ring box. The second note read:

> "Hello, my name is Samson. Will you be so kind and gracious to let me live with you, giving me a happy forever loving home? I am already house broken, been wormed and up to date on all my puppy shots. I promise I will be a very good and protective guard dog for you who will love my master now and forever, unconditionally. Someone had my slobbering glands taken out, so I won't be slobbering all over, like my brothers and sisters do. But that sure hurt me. OWEY! But I'm all healed up from that and doing ok. I can eat like a horse! The guy who led me to you already bought me some puppy food, wet and dry. He mixes it together for me and me really like that! Mmmmmm! Then I eat my dry food off and on all day in between my naps and play times. Please let me be your forever protector because I'm nonrefundable, oh and this little red velvet box is for you. But I was told to tell you NOT TO OPEN IT until the guy who put it around my neck, shows up. I think he said his name was Jesse. He told me he loves you very much. Thank you, in advance for giving me a wonderful, loving home, and mommy. Can I call you mommy? I promise I will be the best dog you'll ever have and to be very proud of. I love you mommy!"

Michelle looked up from reading the note to find Jesse walking up to the porch with Samson's leash. Samson licked her on her face as she'd be laughing and crying at the same time. She put Samson down and ran down the stairs to meet Jesse with open arms and hugged him so tightly. Jesse took the red velvet box from Michelle's hand and opened it to show a beautiful, 24k gold heart-shaped diamond engagement ring. More tears would be streaming down her face, as he took the ring out of the box; Jesse bent down on one knee and slipped it on her finger.

"Michelle Renee' Mertz, will you please give me the honor and pleasure and marry me and be my one and only true love?"

"Oh Jesse, yes, yes I will marry you, Mr. Jesse Lee Fox, I will. I surely will. I have waited for you for so long."

Michelle leaned over to kiss Jesse as he was still on his knee and lost her balance, falling into his arms and causing both of them to fall onto the grass laughing. Samson licked both of their faces, jumping on them, wanting to play.

Chapter Twelve

As the next few weeks pass, Michelle was busy planning their wedding. She just couldn't fathom she was actually marrying the man of her dreams. Her life was beginning to take on real meaning, with her book getting published and made into a movie, now being engaged to the most wonderful man in her dreams.

Michelle and Dawn were sitting outside on her front porch swing, looking through bridal magazines and watching Danielle and Jacob play with Samson.

"Oh, this is cute for Danielle. What do you think? And this dress for me?"

"Yea, I like both of them, but I like these better." Michelle pointed at a she was looking at.

"You know my dress is going to have an open heart design on it either on the front or back, plus a heart on the train."

"Did you find someone to make your dress?"

"Yes. Mrs. Twins, our Home Economics teacher from high school."

"Oh wow! That's cool! Where did you run into her?"

"I just went up to the high school one day last week and asked her if she'd make it. I told her I'd pay her, plus buy the material and sequence I wanted on it."

"Well, that was nice of her. I always liked her. She was nice."

Michelle's cell phone rings and Dawn gets up and walked out by the gated pasture to watch the kids playing with Samson. When Michelle finished her call, she walked out by the fence where Dawn was.

"Hey, I never paid you and Jake for taking care of things around here when I hurt my ankle. And I was thinking of taking Danielle and Jacob for a weekend so you and Jake can spend some quality time together. You two need that, especially now because of what happened with you and Dr. Viza, you know? How are things between you and Jake?"

"Okay. We have our moments, but I think everything is good between us. And I told you that you didn't have to owe us anything for doing that. We were glad to help you out in your time of need. That's what true friends are all about. We are like family. How is your ankle by the way? Is it all healed up and good as new?"

"Yes it is, thank you, but quit changing the subject. Why don't you and Jake plan this weekend, going out to your cabin by the lake or that place where you stayed on your honeymoon? And I will not take NO for an answer. UNDERSTOOD?" Dawn looked at her smiling; shaking her head no and Michelle swatted her on the butt.

"Okay, okay. I'll talk to Jake tonight and see what he says. I will let you know. Who was on the phone?"

"The Macafey's. They have decided to stay down there until the house sells. Then come back and do all the stuff they need to do. They sure have a good time ministering and building churches. She said people are so hungry for God's Word that there that they have standing room only. There have been 78 people saved and filled with the Holy Ghost. Praise God!"

"Michelle, I know you have told me before, but what exactly is the Holy Ghost again?"

"Well, It was explained to me this way. An egg has three parts. There is the shell, the egg white clear part and the yellow yolk. Some people use the egg whites. Others use the yellow yolk, but some people use all three, like the Trinity. Father God, Jesus, God's Son, and The Holy Ghost, which was explained to me as a Helper. When we pray in The Holy Ghost, in tongues or in other words, God's language. He's like our Helper, Who prays for us when we don't know what or how to pray in English. Kinda like our personal lawyer, pleading our case to God. The Holy Ghost or some people refer to Him as the Holy Spirit too, is our Comforter as well. Jesus told His disciples He would send them a Comforter because Jesus was going to ascend back up to Heaven to be seated at the right hand of our Heavenly Father God after He died and rose again on the third day. After Jesus went to Heaven, He sent the Holy Ghost to comfort them so they wouldn't be sad."

"Hmm, I'm starting to understand a little I think. So it's Jesus in us, praying to God for us when we don't have the words to pray. Is that right?"

"Yea, exactly! You are beginning to understand. I'm so proud of you Dawn! And when the Holy Ghost prays for us, there is no doubt that God's perfect and divine Will, will be done, and not our own will. We all should want God's perfect and divine will in our lives because HE is the All-Mighty, All Powerful, All Loving, Who wants the very best for us."

Michelle could tell Dawn was really listening and taking everything in that she was saying. Dawn was getting closer to God, Michelle thought and she'd be another sheep found and out of Satan's filthy little hands. Praise God.

"So that is so nice of Mrs. Twins to make your wedding dress. How much is she charging you?"

"Well, she said that I would have to help her. We are going to look for patterns together next Saturday if you want to go?"

"Okay, sure I want to go! Do you think we could go shopping for a dress for me too? And are you going to let me pick out the style of dress I want to wear as your Matron of Honor?"

"Who said you were going to be my Matron of Honor? As I recall, you weren't too keen on Jesse and I hooking up together, remember?"

"Yea, but since then, haven't I treated him with utmost respect and not bad-mouthed him even once. I actually have been having a lot of fun with you two, double dating, the last few weeks."

"Really? That really means a lot to hear you say that sis. Thank you. I can't believe we are actually getting married in less than a year!" Dawn looked at her phone to see what time it was.

"Oh, I better go pick up my kids from school! I will talk to you later Michelle."
"Okay, be careful. ``I love you."

"Love you too sis. Bye."

Later that evening, Jesse came over, bringing diner from their favorite Chinese Café'. And as always, Samson was right there, begging for a hand out.

"Oh Samson, you are not starving. I just fed you. Go play with your toys."

Michelle tossed his rope across the living room floor as he ran to fetch it.

"Are you still enjoying him my Love?"

"Oh yes! Most definitely! I wouldn't trade him for anything! Even though he has chewed up my favorite pair of sandals, knocked down the shower curtain twice, while I was taking a shower and got into the trash can. The silly pup. He kept on barking, wanting to take a shower with me I guess?"

"Well, I can't say that I blame him. I'd want to take a shower with you too and I don't like it when you are out of my sight either."

"Awe...thanks, Darlin."

Michelle leaned over to kiss Jesse before Samson came back from getting his rope. Michelle pulled away.

"Come here, Jesse replied. I wasn't finished kissing you yet."

Jesse kissed her again, caressing her neck with his fingertips. Michelle loved when he did this, relaxing her every being. Samson brought the rope back, jumping up on the sofa in between Jesse and Michelle, as Jesse was forced to pull away from Michelle. Samson then got down and sat in front of them watching them. Jesse proceeded to kiss Michelle again and Samson started barking. After a few seconds, Michelle pulled away and Samson stopped barking.

"It appears that Samson is jealous of me. Have you noticed every time we get close or start kissing, he comes around us more and starts barking?"

"Oh Jesse, Samson loves you too. I don't think he's jealous. He just demands our attention all the time, as a child does. He's just a baby, aren't you boy, yes you are."

Michelle rubbed Samson's ears the way he liked her too and then threw the rope again.

"OH, so anyway, after I had put the shower curtain back up, the second time and finished taking my shower, I put Samson in the shower with me, to actually see what he'd do. The crazy thing loved it! He was biting at the water and pawing at it. He absolutely loves the water."

"Hmmm, isn't that something. Samson and I are a lot alike. We both love being with the beautiful woman in our lives, love being next to her all the time whether it be in or out of the water."

They finished eating and Jesse helped her clear away their trash.

"Sweetheart, have you thought anymore about us buying this house? I received a call from the Macafey's earlier. They are not coming back again until someone buys the house in order to save a trip. I told them we were getting married. She was so happy for us and wished us the best. They said if we could sell the house at about the same time we were getting married, that they could attend our wedding. And I surely want them to be here for that."

"Did you ask her if they were going to lower the price anymore?"

"No, because I didn't think you were serious or all that interested in buying it."

"It is awfully big for just the two of us Babe. And all the work we'd have to do on mowing and keeping all of it up. It'd be a lot to consider and I'm not getting any younger. What do you want us to do?"

"I believe you already know what I want. Remember, my book got published and with the sales, I've been getting, my editor and publisher have no doubt in their minds that it will be a Bestseller. And you know what that means. Mucho money Baby!"

Jesse started laughing at her lovingly, putting his arm around her.

"Mucho money, huh? You also realize, don't you, that we will be more in demand for writing more books, leaving more work around here to do."

"We? Are you going to help me write my books, Jesse?"

Jesse just looked at her with his honoree grin, not answering her question.

"And no, what that means is we could afford a couple of good looking farm hands to do all the work around here."

"Well, if we are going to do that, then we can afford a couple cute female handmaid's too, to help us inside the house, doing laundry, cleaning and the like." Jesse challenged her. They often ribbed one another, just to see the other's response, and to see who caved first.

Michelle would raise her eyebrows, with a daring look at him. Jesse would add more flame to the fire.

"They could cook and feed me, us, I mean, while you're slaving away on your numerous bestselling novels."

"Ugh, No! I don't think so Mr. If we did that, we'd have to hire two married couples."

Jesse was laughing so hard he was crying.

"Oh Love, come here."

Michelle walked to the kitchen to get more Tea. When he caught up to her, he put his arms around her and kissed her, assuring her he was only playing, which she knew already but was always glad he was always ready to reassure her that he was.

Samson followed Jesse into the kitchen, jumping up on both of them while they were engaged in a kiss. When they continued kissing, Samson started barking at them again. Michelle pulled away laughing.

"See, he is jealous of me!"

Jesse watched her play with Samson for a few minutes. Michelle was still laughing, rubbing Samson's ears.

"He is just keeping you in line Jess. Making sure you treat me like a queen. Yea, isn't that right boy? You are definitely a mama's boy, aren't you baby. Yea, I love you too."

Samson was licking her arm as if to be saying thank you for rubbing his ears the way he loved so much.

"He's probably still mad at me for having his slobber glands removed."

"Maybe, I don't know. I thought you were only teasing about him being jealous of you, but now I'm beginning to believe you are right."

"Well, as long as you give me more loving than Samson here gets, then I guess I won't be jealous of him."

"Oh, do I detect some already Darlin? Hmm?"

"No, I don't think so...'", Jesse mocked her from earlier, making her laugh again. She kissed Jesse on the lips, then twice and start rubbing his ear lobes like she did Samson's, teasing Jesse.

"Oh, do you like your ears rubbed like this too, baby? And how about this?"

She kissed his lips again before she started kissing his ear lobe, sucking it gently, while lightly caressing his other ear with her fingertips. Jesse was enjoying her touch, with his hands roaming around her tighter, pulling her closer to him. Although Samson continued barking, they ignored him for a brief moment.

"No Samson! No bark! Go lay down now!" Samson hung his head down, with his tail between his legs and walked out of the kitchen.

"That's not a bad idea, lying down," Jesse whispered in her ear, caressing Michelle's back slowly, making her lose all concentration.

"Babe, we've talked about this, even though you make it awfully tempting to give in." Michelle pulled away, looking at him.

"I'm sorry, but I want you so bad my Love. I know we both want to honor God and not defile the marriage bed anymore, but oh how very tempting you are to me..."

Jesse passionately kissed her, kiss her neck which was one of Michelle's most sensitive spots. He worked his way down to the top of her blouse, kissing lightly and back up again, ending it with another passionate kiss.

"I better go now before we give in."

Michelle took his hand and pushed it between her thighs, tempting him that much more as she started to reach towards his most sensitive spot.

"Hum, Michelle Love, please don't. We have been abstaining pretty well lately. Let's continue even though it is very difficult."

"Just how "difficult" is it, Jesse...?"

Jesse chuckled as Michelle would catch him off guard and pull away from him, being able to brush up against his hardness.

Chapter Thirteen

The next morning, Jesse sat beside her in bed, reading the newspaper.

"Good morning beautiful. How did you sleep?"

"Mm, I hadn't slept that well in a long time. How about you?"

"I slept like a log." Jesse bent down to kiss her.

"Where is Samson?"

"Oh, he's outside chasing around somewhere. I fed him and played with him for a while when I got here this morning."

"You did? I didn't even hear you come in. What time did you get here?"

"It was a few minutes after 8 this morning. I was trying to be quiet so as not to wake my beautiful princess. I cooked our breakfast, waiting for you to wake up, but you kept sawing those logs."

"I have you know Mr. Fox that I don't snore."- Jesse gave her another kiss.

"Oh yes my Love, but you look so adorable when you're doing it."

"Jesse Lee Fox! You can be so full of it sometimes. The breakfast you cooked, better be mouth-watering delicious, or I'm not going to forgive you for the snoring comment."

Jesse laughed as he gave her another kiss, then another.

"Or would you rather pick up where we left off last night?"

"As tempting as it still is, I need to go pee, and I'm starving."

"Your wish is my command, my Love." Jesse left to go prepare their breakfast plates, and reheating it in the microwave and pouring their coffee and orange juice.

"Mmmmmm Jess, sure smells great, whatever it is."

"I present to you, my specialty omelet, with everything but the kitchen sink in it."

"And just what is in it?"

"Bacon, onions, garlic, cilantro, mushrooms, Velveeta cheese, green bell peppers, red bell peppers, green chilies, and seasonings."

"Wow! I can't wait to dig in." Michelle took Jesse's hand and began to pray over the food.

"Dear Heavenly Father, we thank You for this food we are about to devour, and we ask that You bless it for the nourishment of our bodies. Also thank You, for this beautiful day You have made and we shall rejoice and be glad in it. One more thing Daddy God. We ask You to forgive our fleshly desires as well and please give us Your supernatural strength to overcome and give in to temptation. We thank You and give You all the glory, honor and praise You so rightly deserve daily, in Jesus name, Amen."

"Amen!"

They began to eat their breakfast.

"Oh honey, this omelet is oh so magnificently mouthwatering delicious! Mmmmm"

"Well thank you. I'm so glad you like it. I wasn't sure if you would or not. I couldn't remember if you liked all the stuff I put in it. Oh and I gave the horses freshwater and their oats and fresh hay as well."

"Well, look at you. You're a handy man to have around. I believe I'm going to enjoy being your wife."

"I aim to please honey and fulfill your every wish, Michelle." Jesse took a bite of his food winking at her.

"I've been thinking more about buying this house. When you talk to the Macafey's again, ask them if they would possibly consider lowering the price. If they do, depending on how much they lower it, I'll seriously contemplate on buying it for us."

"Really? Oh Jesse. I'd absolutely love it! Thank you."

"Now, don't thank me yet, until we see for sure. But I gave it some more thought turning this into a weekend getaway house. We could rent it out to people; maybe get a few more horses too, so families with kids can have the pool and horseback riding. And couples who don't have kids can enjoy that too, plus the hot tub."

"Well, yeah. We could do that, maybe. Jesse, this food is delicious! I think you were a chef somewhere in your lifetime because any food you cook is so GOOD!"

Jesse started laughing.

"Well, thank you Babe. But I assure you, I wasn't."

"Then that's even better. It just comes natural to you then. I need to take cooking lessons from you sometime."

"Back to buying the house. We will just have to see. Talk to the Macafey's first and then we will discuss it further."

They finished eating and Jesse took their tray back into the kitchen. Michelle took a shower while Jesse cleaned up the kitchen. After Jesse finished cleaning he poked his head in the bathroom door and told her goodbye, that he had to leave to go pick up his granddaughter from work.

"I don't get a kiss goodbye?" Michelle said, poking her wet head out from the shower curtain. He came in and gave her a kiss.

"I love you, Hon. Be careful and don't work too hard."

"I love you too Sweetheart and you be careful too. Have a nice day! Hey, let me cook dinner for you tonight since you cooked breakfast, okay?"

"Sounds good."

"What shall I fix?"

"I don't know. Surprise me."

"Okay, it'll probably be a surprise alright!"

"No it won't. Whatever it is, it will be wonderful. I'm sure of it."

"I'm glad you are!"

"Okay Love, bye. I will call you later."

He gave her one last kiss and darted out the door. Michelle finished her shower and got ready for work. Her work day went fast, being the first of the month. This usually included people with Access cards, women with WIC, and the elderly with their Social Security checks. Michelle was more than ready to go home and get ready for the weekend, even though it was only Thursday.

Before she left work that day, she bought some things for dinner that she was planning for Jesse. She picked up a roast, onions, mushrooms, garlic, and potatoes. She also picked up some roasting bags and ingredients for the salad. At the bakery, she picked up some oatmeal cookies for dessert. She went home, prepared her pot roast, and placed it in the oven on low. She then prepared the salad before she took a relaxing bath.

It was thirty minutes later when the phone rang and woke her up. She couldn't believe she had fallen asleep in the bathtub! She sprang out of the water, grabbed her towel, and answered the phone breathlessly.

"Hello?" "Honey... Are you okay? Why are you out of breath?"

"I was in the tub and had to run to get the phone. I forgot to bring it with me. How was your day?"

"It was okay. Busy. I worked around the house, getting some things done that I needed to get done. I fixed my garbage disposal, and did my laundry."

"Oh, sounds like fun. I had a busy day too. The first of the month is always busy. Are you ready for your dinner I prepared for you?"

"You bet! What did you cook for us, my Love?"

"You told me to surprise you, so I'm not going to tell you. You will just have to wait."

"Oh I see. Playing that game, are we?"

Michelle started laughing. Then he started to laugh too.

"Well I will see you soon. Do you want me to pick up anything? Maybe a movie or two?"

"Sure that'd be great. Why are you so good to me Jesse?"

"Well, because I love you and because you are the love of my life. I told you last night that you'll never want for anything and I mean that. You mean so much to me Michelle. Please don't ever forget that."

There was a pause before Michelle responded to him.

"Jesse, it scares me when you tell me things like that."

"Why?

"Because, It makes me think that I'm going to lose you again."

There was a silent pause.

"Hon, are you there?"

"Yes, I'm here. I was wiping away tears."

"I'm not ever going to leave you Michelle my love. Please stop worrying. I'm getting very hungry. I will see you soon. I love you, Bye."

They hung up the phone and Michelle got dressed. She checked on the pot roast, which was about ready. She set the table, putting the plates, silver wear, and two glasses with ice on the table. Then she got the salad out and set it on the table with the salad dressing along with the salad dressing, bacon bits, and croutons. Michelle checked the roast again and turned it on warm, seeing that it was done cooking. When she finished at the stove, she sat down at the table and looked out the window. She was watching Samson chase some poor rabbit across the field when Jesse drove up the driveway. She ran to greet him.

After they both enjoyed the delicious dinner, they started cleaning up the kitchen. The telephone rang and it was the Macafey's.

"Hello?"

"Hello Michelle. Have you sold the house yet Honey?"

"No, not yet Mrs. Macafey. But I have a question to ask a favor really. Um, could you consider lowering the price again, if Jesse and I were to buy it?"

"Well, Glory be to God! George and I have been praying and fasting about that very subject, and we called to tell you that we believe God has spoken to us. It was prophesied over us that if we came down on the price that a buyer would come forth."

"Wow!"

"Oh Michelle, that's so nice not having to worry about the olé' place anymore. How much can you and him afford Honey?"

"I'm not sure. But Jesse was talking about maybe turning this place into a Bed and Breakfast."

"Oh! That sounds like a Marvelous idea, Dear! Let me talk it over with George and I'll call you back."

Michelle hung up the phone and told Jesse was she had said.

"Oh and she thought your idea was marvelous."

"She did?"

"Yea, she will get back to us after she talks it over with her husband."

Jesse looked to her and smiled.

"Would you like another refill of Pepsi, my darling?"

"Just half full, please. Thank you. I picked up those movies that we talked about wanting to see the other night.

"Oh, good, I was hoping you wouldn't forget. You are just amazing. You know that?"

"I was just thinking the same thing about you, my Love."

He winked at her before he stood up from the table, capturing her in his arms, planting a kiss on her soft, sexy lips.

"Mmmmmm, thank you for such a delicious dinner. You cook pretty well. The meat was so tender and juicy."

'You are more than welcome. Thank you, for the compliment. I'm glad you enjoyed it."

Chapter Fourteen

As they were going to the sofa, Michelle puts in one of the movies before sitting next to Jesse. The phone rings and Jesse answers the phone."

"Hello."

"Mr. Fox, it's Mrs. Macafey. How are you?"

"Fine, fine Mrs. Macafey. How are you guys doing? I've been hearing from Michelle of the great services you've been having."

"Oh yes, yes Dear. We sure have. People here are so hungry for the Work of God that we have standing room only in most of our services. Glory be to God! So, Michelle tells me you want to make our house into a Bed and Breakfast. I think that is a great idea, Dear. I talked to George and we strongly believe God told us to lower the price by 12,000 dollars. Jesse was in shock but delighted.

"Mrs. Macafey, are you sure you two want to come down THAT much? That is quite a lot. I feel like I'd be stealing it away from you."

"Not at all; we are quite sure about the amount. We have been praying and fasting the last couple of weeks on this matter. We believe God is in this. When do you want to sign the papers, Mr. Fox?"

"Hum, well, anytime that if good for you all. We want you both to attend our wedding, and that's not for a few months yet. How about then?"

"Okay, Mr. Fox, consider it done. Ask Michelle if she'd cancel our ad in the paper for us. Thank you for taking this burden off of our hands, and we'll be praying for you and Michelle too."

"Well I'm the one who owes you both a million thanks. Now, are you absolutely positive about this?"

"Oh yes, yes Honey, we are. Now, stop fussing and thank the Good Lord for it. We will be talking to you later about the arrangements. God bless you honey and Michelle too. Bye!"

Jesse hung up the phone, as Michelle was anxiously waiting to hear what she said.

"Well Love, we have ourselves a B&B, if we decide to do it."

"Really? I knew it! Praise God! Thank you Jesus! Glory! God is awesome Jesse!"

"Yes, yes He is! Thank YOU, Heavenly Father, thank YOU!"

Jesse took Michelle in his arms and hugged her tightly for a long time. After a few seconds, Michelle felt a tear run down her arm and she pulled away from Jesse to look at him.

"Jess, what is it?"

Michelle wiped away his tear from his other eye as he looked into hers.

"God IS so good to me, Michelle, and I am just now really realizing it, more and more these past few weeks. And what have I don't for HIM? I can't tell you of anything that I have done for HIM. Nothing, and yet, HE still continues to bless me. I feel His All Holy presence around both of us right now. His love, His unconditional love, Oh I can't explain it. I want to go to church with you Sunday. Not just this Sunday, but every time, all the time."

Michelle was crying too, as Jesse wiped her tears away also, and they both started laughing.

"You've asked Jesus into your heart, haven't you Jesse? I always knew you believed in God, but didn't know if you accepted HIM into your heart and had a personal relationship with Him. But I do believe you have now. Am I right?"

"Yes, I have. Ever since you had told me about that white haired preacher on TV, I have been watching him, almost every time he comes on, along with reading the Bible, too. When he was on last night, I asked Jesus to come into my heart and to be the Lord of my life. I want to thank you too, for introducing me to Brother Gene, and for being a witness before me as well. I love you Michelle, as Jesus loves us."

As they embraced again, the movie started to play. They watched their movies the rest of the evening and Jessie left to go home. Michelle does her nightly routine, getting ready for bed, then she kneels down on her knees, talking to God that night, before she went to bed and fell asleep.

The next morning, she got up feeling so happy and blessed. She was so excited that Jesse got saved and he told her, the way he told her, and seeing God's Holy Power all over him. It was just awesome. She would never forget it as long as she lived.

The day flew by at work, as she kept busy with customers. It was finally the weekend, and as she promised Donna, her two children stayed with her, while her and Jake went off for the weekend. That evening, she and Jesse took the kids to the amusement park. When they got up the next morning, Michelle fixed them their favorite breakfast.

"Okay, kids, are you ready for some chocolate chip pancakes, some rodeo steak, and chocolate milk to wash it all down with?"

"Yea!' the kids said in unison.

"Thank you Aunt Michelle, for fixing us breakfast. Our favorite breakfast, in all of the world."

"You're welcome Jacob."

"Danielle, tell Aunt Michelle thank you."

"Thank you Aunt Michelle. ''I love you."

"Oh, honey, I love you too. You are welcome."

Michelle loved Donna's kids as if they were her very own. She had taken care of them on different occasions when Donna and Jake needed her to. She was like their second mom. She was there when they both were born, and at all their birthday parties too. As Michelle was watching them eat, thinking back on those happy memories, Jessie would know on the door and come in, bringing the kids each a toy, and Michelle a beautiful vase with 3 red roses in it.

"Good morning beautiful." And he kissed her.

"What are these for? They are beautiful, and the vase too. Thank you Babe."

"You are welcome. And these, are for you two."

"Thank you Jesse. Aunt Michelle, can we play with them now?"

"I thought you could play with them in the pool this afternoon, when we get back from the zoo."

Jesse looked at Michelle lovingly, winking at her, then back at the kids.

"Are we going to the zoo?" Danielle asked.

"I guess we are now, kids. What do you tell Jesse?"

"Thank you," they both said in unison, again.

When they all finished eating, Michelle and the kids got dressed to go to the zoo. Jesse was cleaning up the kitchen when Michelle came in.

"Jesse, you didn't have to clean my mess up, thank you. You are just being really sweet today. I mean, you are real sweet all the time, but today you are sweeter than normal, what's up?"

Jesse chuckled wiping off the stove.

"Does there have to be something up for me to be extra sweet to my precious Love of my life?"

"Well, no. I just haven't seen you this cheerful and so loveable. Ever since you go saved, I sure have been seeing a side of you I am really growing to love you more and more."

"Oh, is that so?"

Michelle took the dishcloth away from him and wipe off the table, go to the sink and wash it out. After she folded it and laid it on the sink to dry, she turned around to Jesse and kissed him.

"Yes, that is definitely so."

"Well that's good that you like this side of me, because I intend to show it more often. I can't wait to be your husband, Michelle. You deserve the very best from me for putting up with me all these years."

"Oh Jesse, it wasn't too hard. The only hard part was not being able to see or talk to you after I graduated."

"Okay, Aunt Michelle, we are ready to go to the zoo."

"Alright, Ask Jesse if he is ready."

"Are you ready to go to the zoo now?"

"You bet I am!"

Jesse picked Danielle up and kiss her on the cheek as they all got into Jesse's car and took off for the zoo. As promised, when they arrived back home they went swimming.

"Aunt Michelle, watch me! I'm going to do a backflip off the diving board! Watch!" Jacob yelled.

"Jacob, you be careful!"

Splash! Jacob bounced up out of the water laughing.

"That was fun! I'm going to do it again!"

"Oh, no you are not, young man! Once is quite enough. Why don't you slide down the slide with your little sister?"

"Oh, do I have to? The slide is for babies!"

"Jacob, prease. Pretty prease whiff sugar on top?" Danielle begged.

"How old are you, Jacob?" Jesse asked.

"I'm seven and Danielle is three. Why?"

"And you think the slide is for babies, huh?"

"Oh, okay, but just this once. Come here Danielle."

Jacob slid down the slide with Danielle, being careful with her as he always was, with Danielle laughing all the way. Michelle caught her and hugged her tightly.

"Did you like that sweetie?"

"Let's do it again!"

"No I'm going off the diving board again. That's for big kids like me."

"Oh, is that so Mr. Jacob? Watch this!"

Jesse took Danielle from Michelle and slid down the slide with her in his arms, making a big splash.

"Well, you wouldn't slide down by yourself because…" Jacob blurted out.

And Jesse proved him wrong, sliding down the slide without Danielle.

"How about that?"

Jacob was surprised, and started laughing, as Danielle was clapping her hands. Michelle was laughing too, not believing he did it.

"Oh, and just what are you laughing at missy? Hmm? Come here you sexy thing. Come here. I'm going to teach you a lesson too."

Jesse grabbed her arm and pulled her out of the water, dragging her to the steps of the slide. Both kids were sitting on the steps in the water cheering Jesse on, laughing.

"No Jesse, no! Jesse!"

"It's either you slide down or being thrown in. Take your pick."

Jesse was laughing so hard, he lost his grip on Michelle and she got away.

"You can't get away that easy. Come back here. Looks like you picked to be thrown in, didn't you?"

Jesse caught up to her, picked her up, and carried her to the deepest part of the pool.

The kids were cheering and laughing.

"Okay, kids, help me count."

Jesse swung Michelle back and forth.

All in unison they counted.

"One!"

"Jesse! Don't you do it!"

"Two!"

"Jesse! I'm warning you!"

"Three!"

Jesse jumped in with her, not throwing her in by herself, after all.

"Awe, you should have thrown her in Jesse, by herself!"

"Okay Jacob. I will remember that when you want me to fix breakfast again."

They all laughed, enjoying the company they were in, and the wonderful day they all were having. Before the swimming was finished, Michelle managed to push Jesse off into the deep end, even though he didn't toss her into the water. Then Jesse forced her to slide down the slide, squirting her with one of the kids' water guns he got them that morning.

"Now, see. It wasn't all that bad, now was it, Aunt Michelle?"

"Jesse Lee Fox! I was almost dried before you forced me to do that!"

The kids were laughing with Jesse.

"So you see kids. Slides are not just for babies. They are for grown-ups too, aren't they Aunt Michelle?"

Jesse slid down the slide again.

"Aunt Michelle, will you slide down the slide with me, prease?"

Danielle looked at Michelle, batting her big blue eyes at her. Then Michelle looked at Jesse, as he'd be laughing all the more.

"Look what you started. Sure honey, come one. Aunt Michelle will you take you down the slide."

They slid down the slide together, laughing.

After enjoying their swimming, they went in and got cleaned up. They all created an appetite, so Jesse grilled some hot dogs for the kids and a couple of steaks for Michelle and him. Michelle prepared some veggies and hot rolls while the kids were busy setting the table, waiting for Jesse to bring in the rest of the meal.

It was nearing 9:00 and the kids were still up, playing with Samson.

"Kids, it's bed time now. Go get your PJ's on and brush your teeth. Jesse and I will be in to tuck you in. Oh, be sure and use the restroom too before you get in bed."

"Okay, Aunt Michelle. Jesse, can we start calling you Uncle Jesse, since you two are getting married?"

"Jacob that would be an honor. I'd be pleased as punch if you two called me Uncle Jesse."

89

"Uncle Jesse?"

"What is Sugar Plum?"

"That's not my name. Why did you call me that?"

Michelle and Jesse started laughing.

"Danielle, it's just a pet name. You know, like I call you Sweetie, sometimes."

"Oh, okay. But Uncle Jesse, how is punch pleased? You said you would be pleased as punch if we called you Uncle Jesse."

They all laughed at her again, as Jesse picked her up and hugged her.

"It's just an expression Sugar Plum. Something people say when they can't find the words to show how they feel. So they say silly sayings like that to let people know how they feel."

"Oh."

While the kids were getting ready for bed, Michelle stole a kiss from Jesse.

"Mm, what was that for?"

"Oh, it was just because kiss, and this one is because I love you. And this one is because you are so wonderful to me, and have been so terrific with the kids this weekend."

"I've had a lot of fun this weekend."

"I know. I could tell."

"We are ready Aunt Michelle and Uncle Jesse."

"Okay, we are on our way."

Chapter Fifteen

*M*ichelle and Jesse tucked Danielle and Jacob in as promised. Michelle bent down to kiss Danielle goodnight, tucking her in good and tight, doing the same to Jacob.

"There. You both are as snug as a bug in a rug. Good and tight. Now, I'll be getting you both up early for Sunday school. And I will have your clothes laid out for you. Did you say your prayers?"

"Yep, I did"

"That's good, Tiger."

"I did, too."

"Okay, I love you both. Sweet dreams."

"Uncle Jess. Are you going to church with us?"

"You bet. I wouldn't miss it for the world. I'll pick y'all up in the morning, around 9:30."

"Okay, Good night. Sleep tight, and don't let the bedbugs bite."

Jacob started laughing

"That's another one of those silly sayings people say, isn't it Uncle Jesse?"

"Yes, Sugar Plum, it is. It's just another silly saying."

"You're silly, Uncle Jesse. Goodnight!"

Michelle turned out the light and they walked in the living room to sit down to relax, before Jesse left to go home.

"Those kids are really smart for their ages. Danielle really reminds me a lot of Barbie, when she was that age."

"They really are smart. Dawn does a good job of raising them. Jake does too. They are good parents."

"Well, it looks like you had a lot to do with their upbringing too."

While they were kissing on the couch, Danielle came out into the living room.

"Aunt Michelle, I'm firsty."

"Okay Honey. I'll get you a drink of water."

Michelle got up getting her the glass of water, as she finished the whole glass, then she went back to bed. A few minutes later she was up again.

"I have to go to the bathroom."

"Okay Danielle, but after this you get back into bed and go to sleep, okay? You don't want to be sleepy in Sunday school, do you?"

"No."

"Okay, see you in the morning."

After she used the bathroom, she came and hugged Michelle and Jesse goodnight one last time.

"Goodnight, Aunt Michelle and Uncle Jesse. I wuv you."

"We love you too."

"Okay Sugar Plum. You better go to bed and shut those peepers of yours, so you won't fall asleep in church."

Danielle then obeyed, slowly going back to bed, and stayed there for the rest of the night. Michelle fixed them a glass of iced tea and they sat outside on the porch swing, enjoying the nice breezy night air.

"Wow! It's been 30 minutes and no peep from the kids. You know, they really seem to like you, Babe."

"Well, I really like them too!"

Michelle was still so amazed that she was with the man of her dreams. And now, knowing that he was saved just made her more aware that this was definitely meant to be.

Sunday came and Jesse arrived right on time. They went to church and Michelle introduced him as her best friend and fiancé. Some people knew him already and others were glad to meet him. Her Pastor knew him too and was so happy he finally came to church with her. As they were singing the songs and hymns, Michelle heard Jesse singing. She was impressed that he knew some of the songs. And the ones he didn't know, he followed along in the book. When it came time to pray, Michelle heard him praying too. And when it came time to give tithes and offerings, he gave his tithes and offerings.

Michelle was so impressed by what she was seeing and hearing from him, that she wanted to shout out loud. She thanked and praised God for answering her prayers and just knew, God had big plans for Jesse. She knew God fill him up with the Holy Ghost and use him for HIS Glory, all the way.

After church was over, Brother and Sister Garfield, the Pastors, asked them to go out to lunch with them.

"If you guys don't have any other plans, we would like to invite you out to lunch with us."

"That is awful nice of you guys, but can we take a rain check? We have to get these kids back to their parents. They are coming home this afternoon and we promised them we'd give them a short horseback ride before then. '' Michelle answered Brother Perry.

"Oh, well okay. We will do it some other time then."

"Michelle, you be careful on those horses now. We don't want you falling again". Sister Perry mothered her, as she always did.

"Okay. I will be careful."

"I'll be there to watch out for her. You will see us tonight."

"Alright, Brother Jesse. I'm going to hold you to that." Brother Perry insisted.

"You can count on it."

They picked up the kids from their classes and drove off.

"Who's hungry?"

"I am! I am!" both kids shouted.

"How about you, Love? Where should we go for lunch?"

"Mickey D's! Mickey D's!"

"If you ask Uncle Jesse nicely, he might take you there."

"Uncle Jesse? Could we? Could we go to McDonald's for lunch, please?"

"Yeah, can we, prease, prease, pretty prease, whif sugar on top?"

"Now, how on Earth could I turn down and refuse? Sure we can."

He turned into McDonald's and they went inside to order. The kids asked if they could eat outside by the play yard."

"Yes, but you have to wait for us first. Do you want chicken Happy Meals?"

"I do! Whiff a Dr. Pepper."

"Jacob, what do you want?"

"I want a Big Mac, French fries, and a Dr. Pepper."

"Can you eat all of that?"

"Mom gets them for me all of the time and I can eat most of it."

"Well, okay then, Jesse, here is some money for the kids and I. I want a salad with ranch and a tea."

"No, put your money away. I got this."

"Jesse prease, whiff sugar on top?"

Michelle mocked Danielle and look up at him, blinking her eyes. Jesse laughed at her, but still not taking her money, telling her to go sit down. Michelle took the kids to the restroom, while they were waiting on their order. When they had finished, they all met outside to eat their lunch.

"Who wants to pray over the food, Jacob?"

"No."

"I do!"

"Okay Danielle, go ahead."

She and the others bowed their heads as she began to pray.

"God is good. God is great. And thank you for this food. Amen."

"Amen, Sweetheart, that was wonderful. Where did you learn that from?"

"In Sunday school this morning. The teacher brought us donuts and orange juice, and she asked a kid to pray over the food and that's what he said."

"Well that's great, Danielle. What else did you learn?"

"About a big oh whale that swallowed up a boy!"

"Jonah and the whale."

"Yeah, Jonah. That was his name."

"Jacob, what did you learn?" Jesse asked.

"About Jesus being a fisherman. But he was a fisherman of people too, not just fish."

"That's right Jacob. Very good! I'm proud of both of you."

"Sounds like you two listened very well and learned a lot. I'm proud of you kids as well. Maybe your mom and dad will come to church with us sometime. We just need to continue to pray for God to help and guide them and for Jesus to put the desire in their hearts to want to come to church with us."

When they finished eating, they let the kids play in the play yard for a little while, then they went home, going horseback riding.

Dawn and Jake arrived around 4 p.m. to pick up the kids. Michelle was very pleased to see Dawn and Jake looking as if they thoroughly enjoyed their weekend together, walking with their arms around each other like they did in high school. Praise God, Michelle thought. The kids ran up to their parents excitedly, hugging them.

"Hi Mommy and Daddy! We rode the horses!"

"You did? Were you two good for Aunt Michelle?"

"Yes, they behaved like perfect little angels."

Dawn and Jake started laughing.

"Oh, I bet they did," Dawn said.

"I have a hard time believing that one. What else did you guys do this weekend?", Jake asked them.

"We went to the zoo yesterday and to Dollywood on Friday!", Jacob exclaimed happily.

"Wow! Sounds like Aunt Michelle spoiled you two more rotten than you are now."

"And we went swimming and to church too! Uncle Jesse bought us water guns and slid down the slide whif me! That was so fun! Will you go to church whif us sometime, Mommy and Daddy? Preeze?" Danielle asked.

"Uncle Jesse?"

"Yes Mommy. Uncle Jesse." Danielle pointed to Jesse as he was walking up from the barn.

"Hey you two. How was your weekend? Was it as fun as ours?" Jesse asked them both, as he stretched out his hand to Jake.

"We asked him if we could call him Uncle Jesse since he was marrying Aunt Michelle. And he said yes we could."

"Oh okay. As long as he doesn't mind."

"So, how was y'all's weekend?"

"We had an incredible time," Jake answered.

"Yes, we absolutely did. It was like a second honeymoon all over again!"

"Oh that's great you guys. I'm really glad you two had a great time. You two needed that time together."

"Thank you, you two, for taking care of the rugrats. How can we repay you?"

"No, do not even go there. Just seeing you two happy is well worth it. Besides, I was repaying I'll back for everything you did around here while I was recuperating from my foot injury."

"Well, you didn't have to do that, but thank you again, so much. Jacob and Danielle, are you ready to go home? I'm sure Aunt Michelle and Uncle Jesse are ready for you to."

"We enjoyed having them Dawn, seriously. And yes, they were very good kids. I'm anxious to hear about your weekend." Michelle whispered into Dawn's ear.

Dawn started laughing.

"Oh, do we have to go Mom? I wanted to go swimming again." Jacob asked.

"No, come on now. Give kisses and hugs. We need to go and get our chores done. Maybe Daddy will stop and get us ice-cream before we go home."

"Daddy, can we, can we preeze?"

Dawn and Jesse started laughing.

"I see she pulls on you guys too, huh? She got me with that sweet little voice and big blue eyes too. Didn't you Sugar Plum?"

"Oh yea, she is quite the little charmer when she really wants something." Jake picked Danielle up after she gave hugs and kisses to Dawn and Jesse.

"I reckon we can stop and get ice-cream before we go home."

"Yay!, both Jacob and Danielle shouted in unison.

"Thank you again you two, so much. I'll call you later Michelle."

"Thanks Mr. F., Jake said, shaking his hand again. Thanks a lot."

"Call me Jesse, Jake. We had a good time with the kids. You two really have raised them well. I congratulate you guys. A job well done."

"Thanks, Jesse."

As they were driving off, the kids were waving bye and laughing at Samson chasing after a bird trying to fly, jumping up trying to catch it. Michelle and Jesse walked back up to the house and went inside.

"Do you miss not being able to have children Michelle?"

"At times I do, but then I think God must have a good reason why I had to have a partial Hysterectomy. He knows what's best for us, and I do trust in Him. He knows what He is doing. And He knows all I want is to please Him and His perfect, blessed will in every area of my life."

Jesse looked at her as they sat on the sofa.

"I love you." Jesse told her.

"Awe, I love you too Jess. In fact, I love you more."

"I'm not so sure about that, my Love."

Michelle smiled from ear to ear when Jesse assured her how much he loved her.

"Okay, so it's equal then. We love each other the same."

"Nah, I believe I love you more because I saw you first. That makes me knowing you longer."

"What are you talking about? Are you saying it was love at first sight?"

"Don't you believe in love at first sight Michelle?"

"Not until I saw you for the first time, I didn't."

"See, there you go. I saw you first and the rest is History. So therefore, I love you more."

"Oh I see where you are going with this. Since you saw me first, you have known me longer. Just when and where did you see me first, Mr. Jesse L Fox?"

"Actually, I saw you even before you started high school. You could say, I watched you grow up."

"Really? Now you have my attention, you stocker." Michelle started laughing.

"I used to live in the same neighborhood as you did, before I moved to where I live now."

"Wow! You have never told me this before. Where did you live? Why haven't you told me before now?"

"I don't know. I wasn't trying to keep it from you. I will have to show you where I used to live in the old neighborhood."

"So, when did you notice me? When did you first fall in love with me Jesse?"

Jesse's cell phone sounded off. Before he answered it, he said, "Save by the bell."

Michelle playfully hit him on the arm and then got up, going into the kitchen to get them a glass of iced tea, to give him some privacy. Michelle was standing at the kitchen sink, watching Samson chase some poor rabbit into a hole, and then started barking at the hole, wagging his tail. Michelle started laughing at him and took a drink of her tea. Jesse came up behind her, putting his hands around her waist and started kissing her neck.

"Mmmmmm..., Jesse, you know you make me crazy when you do this."

"Do what my beautiful baby love?"

Jesse turned her around and kiss her neck again, then kisses her passionately before he turned her loose and then he took a drink of her iced tea.

"That was Barbie."

"Oh, is she okay?"

"Oh yea, she's fine. She is doing some research for me on something and she just wanted to call and tell me what she found out."

"Hmm, okay. What are you up to now Jesse?"

"Don't be so suspicious. It could be a surprise for you."

"Jess, I don't need surprises all the time. I'm a big girl now. Besides, I have you now. And you are all the surprise I need in my life. I kept hoping and praying that we'd end up together, and now, just look at us. We are two peas in a pod, stuck together like glue. God has answered my prayers and I will always be extremely thankful to Him for you. Speaking of which, when did you first see me and fall in love?"

"I drove by your house one hot Summer day and you were sunbathing, basking in the hot July sun. You had on a pair of pink sunglasses and a black two piece bikini, with your pretty blonde hair up in a ponytail on the top of your head. I drove by 3 times, just to see your beautiful glistening body. I honked as I drove by the third time."

"Oh my gosh! I remember that! It kinda creeped me out, thinking some perverts spying on me."

"I'm sorry. I didn't mean to "creep you out", as you put it, but you were, and still are, the most beautiful thing I saw and fell in love with you right then and there. And so I made it my mission to find out what your name was and when you got in high school, I made sure you were in my class."

"Wow!"

"Are you surprised?"

"Ugh, yes! You were stalking me!"

"Michelle, please don't do this. I was afraid you'd react this way."

Michelle started laughing out loud like he never heard her laugh before, as tears fell from her eyes.

"Oh Jesse, the look on your face was priceless. Do you honestly think that really matters now? I am so happy you drove by and saw me. Now it would have been creepy, if you'd have stopped and watched me from the curb or something. Offered me candy or whatever, but you didn't."

"I gave you my heart that day and would have given you the moon if it was within my power."

"Awe, well seven more months and I will be yours."

"God, give me strength."

"He will. He doesn't put on us anymore than we can bear, and He also makes away for escape too."

Michelle turned around to face Jesse, as he'd look down, then back up to her. He was putting off what he had to tell her.

"Speaking of a way to escape. Babe, I have to go out of town for a while on business. But I will call you and you can call me. I was hating to tell you because I'm going to miss you so much."

"Where are you going? Is there anything wrong?"

"No Sweetheart, stop worrying. Everything is going to be just fine. I just have to take care of some business is all. And I'll be making money while I'm gone for our honeymoon. Which reminds me, you haven't told me where you want to go yet?"

Michelle was quiet now, looking away from him, with tears streaming down her face.

"Sweetheart, look at me."

Jesse knew her actions well enough to know that she was crying and upset with him.

"Love, come here. I will come back, I promise you that. You can't get rid of me that easy."

He'd hug her against his chest as her tears kept falling.

"I just don't understand why, why you always have to be SO secretive? Why can't you just tell me. Don't you trust me, Jesse?"

"Michelle, please. Don't get upset at me. It will be only for a little while longer, and then we will be together forever. Just you and me. Married, finally. I will tell you everything when I get back. Anything you want to know, I promise."

"'I promise.' Whatever! That's all I've been hearing from you lately, and you haven't told me anything yet!"

She'd look at him, as he'd be wiping her tears away. She pulled away from him, looking at the clock.

"We need to get ready for church."

Michelle got up and went to the bathroom to freshen up. Jesse knew she was really upset with him, but it was for her own good. He loved surprising her with things, and going out of his way to do it. He knew she'd be upset with him, but in the long run, believe she'd forgive him, as she always had done. He also knew within his heart of hearts he'd make it up to her.

They went to church together, even though Michelle didn't say anymore to him, at all, giving him the silent treatment the rest of the evening. When she wasn't signing, Jesses really knew she was upset with him. Micelle loves singing in church, and when she didn't, it meant something was wrong. Either she didn't feel well or as of late, she was mad at Jesse. Brother Garfield had kept the service shorter than usual, so they dismissed early. When they were leaving, Brother Garfield was at the door, shaking everyone's hands and giving hugs.

"Well, take care of Michelle while I'm gone, will you, Brother?"

"While you're gone? Where are you going?"

"Oh, he can't say. He's on another mission from God or something."

Michelle smarted off and walked out the door without giving Sister Garfield a hug first. Sister Garfield walked out after her, while Jesse and Brother Garfield continued talking inside.

"Come here young lady, and give me a hug. What's this all about Michelle?"

"Oh, I don't know. If he keeps up this mystery, secretive crap much longer I don't believe there will be a wedding!"

"Now, Dear. I'm sure it's nothing to get upset over."

She gave her a hug.

"Oh no? Do you know something that I don't? Seems like other people do, when I'm the one who is in the dark all the time!"

Jesse came out the door then, as Michelle walked to the car and got in. On the way home, Michelle continues to give him the silent treatment as she kept her eyes looking out her window. When Jesse pulled up into the drive and turned off the engine, he was really beginning to wonder is Michelle was ever going to talk to him again. He reached over across her shoulder and caressed it. Michelle didn't respond. So he moved closer to her slowly, and started caressing her neck. Michelle's defenses started to break down as she closed her eyes and turned to look at him. She really hated when he get to her like this. He knew, always knew, hot to beat and break down her defenses, and it just wasn't fair she thought.

Still, without a word being said to each other, Jesse pulled her to him, kissing her like never before. It was slow, gentle, but with real passions that said was mere words couldn't. After he kissed her he walked her up to the front door, kissed her again like he had previously, and hugged her real snug for a long time, then he left. Michelle cried herself to sleep that night, and prayed in the Holy Ghost.

Chapter Sixteen

*T*he next few months were hard for Michelle, but she managed to get through them with God's help. Also, with Jesse calling every week made it better too. If he didn't call, he'd email her an I love you, or poem to let her know he missed her as much as she did him.

Michelle had almost all of the wedding plans ready, getting her bridesmaid dress picked out and sized, along with her flower girl and ring bearer dresses and tux fitted. She was having her wedding dress made by her Home Economics Teacher, Mrs. Twins. As Michelle was checking off her wedding To Do list, the telephone rang.

"Hello?"

"Hi, my beautiful Love! How are you?"

"Jess! Hi! I'm great now, since you called! How are you?"

"I'm finer than frog's hair! Things are really going well here. Should be home maybe in a few days."

"Really?! That's great! I really wish I knew just what you were up to Jesse Lee!"

"Hon, I got to run. I love you and I miss you terribly! If only you knew how much! I'll call you again when I have more time. Kisses and hugs!"

"Jesse, I love you and miss you bunches and bookoos too! And thanks for calling and sending those poems! Makes me want you, even more! Please be careful, and take care of yourself. That's an order, Mister!"

"Okay Love, I will. I love you. Talk to you soon. Bye."

Michelle missed him so much, but kept busy working and continues with the wedding plans. It really made her curious what Jesse was up to this time. She didn't know where he was or what he was doing, but somehow she trusted him, and God to watch over and protect him of any danger.

While the days dragged on, Michelle and Mrs. Twins finished her wedding dress. She absolutely loved it. It was her dream dress.

"Okay, Michelle. Go try it on. Let's see how it fits now. If you keep losing weight girl, I don't know what I'm going to do."

"I'm sorry! I just miss my baby, that's all."

Michelle went and tried it on in her bedroom. They usually worked on the dress at Mrs. Twins, but this time they were at Michelle's soon to be house. Michelle's mom, Michelle's two sisters, her niece, Dawn, and Dawn her best friend from work were all there to help her dress for the first time and the final fitting.

"Do you need any help, Money?" her niece Angela asked. She had called her that for years, since Michelle had told her that her Uncle Mark used to call her Money, when she was growing up.

"Yeah, as a matter of fact, I do, Anj. Thanks."

Angela went back to her bedroom to help her. She helped her zip up and put her veil on, when they walked out of the bedroom.

"Wow! It's lovely Michelle!" Dawn said.

"Yeah you look beautiful, Honey," her mom said.

"Michelle I never knew you had it in it. You do look rather nice for being our baby sister. What do you think Marcel?"

"Yea, not too shabby Michelle."

"Well, it looks like everybody approves, Michelle. You do look pretty in it, except for this."

Mrs. Twins pulled a loose string off from the bottom of it

"What do you think, Michelle? Do we need any more adjustments?"

"No, I don't think so. It feels good, looks beautiful, and fits comfortably. I think we finally did it, Mrs. Twins."

"Who did it, Michelle? I don't recall you doing any sewing on it, even though I did teach you in class, years ago"

They all started laughing.

"Angela, you hadn't said anything about it. What do you think?"

"I think it ought to be tea length and camouflage. That's what mine is going to look like."

"Oh Angela, it isn't either."

"Yea it is Grandma. Just you wait and see."

They all started laughing again and Michelle went to change. They all left and had lunch together at Olive Garden.

"Now, we all have to do is wait for my beloved to get himself back here, wherever he is, so we can get his and his best man's tux ordered."

"Who is he having for his best man Michelle?"

"I'm not sure, but he mentioned one of his brothers and a couple of guys he played cards with."

"Have you met his family yet?", her sister Mary asked.

"I have met his lovely granddaughter, Barbie. She's a sweetheart. I remember seeing his daughter and son years ago, but never officially met them. He has a sister and three brothers that I hadn't met that I know of anyway. Knowing him, being so secretive, he has probably sent them in the store to go thru my line to see what they thought of me or whatever."

"How do his kids feel about you marrying their dad?", her mom asked.

"I feel like they are not too happy about it for some reasons, but maybe in time, they will be willing to accept it. I hope so anyway." While Michelle was getting ready to take Dawn out for her birthday, her cell phone sounded off. June 7th, only one month away until the Big Wedding Day, it flashed on her screen, along with this scripture;

James 1:3 *Be assured and understand that the trial and proving of your faith bring out endurance and steadfastness and patience of Christ.*

From the Amplified Bible. Wow, Michelle thought. She couldn't believe only one more month and she will be married to the man of her dreams, finally. Time really does work the patience, she thought. As Michelle finished curling her hair, her phone rang.

"Michelle, this is Mrs. Mainprize, your publisher. I'm calling about your Best Seller, slash movie. Michelle, your book made top ratings on the Bestseller list."

Michelle screamed excitedly.

"Oh my precious God! Thank You Jesus! Thank You God! Thank you too, Mrs. Mainprize! Thank you, Thank you, Thank you!"

"Michelle, please call me Diane. And you wrote the book. I had nothing to do with it. Girl, you ought to be very proud of yourself. Now listen, I had my team here, make it into a screenplay for you. I have already talked to and showed the manuscript to the producers that agreed to do it, but I told him I was going to contact you to look over the manuscript before we started production on it. They loved what they read and anxious to get together with you right away. How soon can you get a flight out to L.A. to look it over?"

"Ugh, ugh… as soon as I possibly can. Oh my gosh! I'll have to make a few calls first. Call my boss at work and let him know. Do you know how long I will be gone, or how long it will take?"

"It's hard to say. It could be a month or several months. It just depends, but you don't have to stay to see the whole movie getting made Michelle."

"Oh, but I want to! I just have to quit my job and my boss will just have to understand. Oh my gosh! I can't believe all this is happening to me!"

"It is quite real Michelle, believe it. You did it girl. You did it."

"Okay, I will come to your office as soon as I arrive. Thank you again, Diane. I will get the next flight to L.A. and call you when I get there."

"You are welcome my friend, but I believe you thanked the right Person to start with, God. I will pick you up at the airport. See you soon."

They hung up the phone and Michelle called her boss. To her surprise, her boss took it rather well. Wasn't too happy that she couldn't finish her week out, but he understood. Michelle called the airport, then Dawn, to tell her sorry her birthday plans got changed, but Dawn was as excited as she was and considered it her birthday present, her book being a best seller and made into a movie. Michelle then called her mom and dad, telling them if Jesse called looking for her to NOT tell him where she was or what she was doing. That she wanted to surprise him, for once, with her big news about her book.

Michelle got ready to go, taking her shower, packing, and trying to stay calm, but it was hard. She just couldn't believe her first book, a best seller, and was also becoming a movie too. She continued to praise God, putting her Bible in her carry on tote. She asked her neighbor to run her to the airport, as the rain delayed the plane a few minutes.

Michelle settled back in her seat, pondering on how great God was. It was HIM that got her this far in life, and especially with her first book becoming a best seller and a movie. She was in awe, in a state of bliss. Michelle took out her Bible and starting reading **Psalm 128. It read:**

Blessed is everyone that feareth the Lord; that walketh in his ways. 2) For thou shalt eat the labor of thine hands; happy shalt thou be, and it shall be well with thee.

Michelle had the joy of the Lord all over her, with tears of happiness flowing down her cheeks. She lifted her hands and started praising God and praying in the Holy Ghost, quietly. When she opened her eyes, after a few minutes, she wiped her eyes, and noticed a young gentleman watching her, offering her a tissue.

"Thank you."

"He must be a good God for you to carry on like that. Hi, I'm Kyle Masters."

"Hi Kyle. Thanks for the Kleenex. I'm Michelle Mertz. And yes, God is SO awesome! He has been good to me, all of my life."

"My dad is a preacher, and wants me to follow in his footsteps. I just don't know about all the stuff, you know? I was raised up in church all of my life, and I have seen a lot."

"Well, Kyle, you know what God's Word says, '' Train up a child in the faith, and when he is old, he will not depart from it. Paraphrased, of course."

"Yes, I know. It's just that there is so much evil in this old world that I just don't understand why God allows it to happen."

"Kyle, let's look at some scriptures, shall we? It says here in Isiah 40:1 and 2:

Comfort ye, comfort ye my people, saith your God. And verse 2: Speak ye comfortably to Jerusalem, and cry unto her, that her warfare is accomplished, that her iniquity is pardoned: for she hath received of the Lord's hand double her sins."

"So, God is punishing the ones who commit sins, right?"

Yea, I believe so. He judges us here on Earth, and he will do the final judgement up in Heaven. Just continue to study His Holy Word Kyle, and trust Him. He still has everything under control, I assure you. Even when we doubt Him at times, or when things look so terrible in our lives, just lean on Him, go to Him in prayer, and

He will be glad to assure you Himself. Just listen with your heart. God and your dad would be so proud of you, doing the work of God! I wish you the very best, and I will be praying for you too."

"It sure was nice talking to you, Michelle, is it? Thanks for the encouragement, and for showing me the scriptures. It meant a lot. So, that's enough about me. What brings you on the plane? I'm flying home to spend time with my dad."

"Oh, that's nice. I'm so excited Kyle! I'm on my way to L.A. to see my first novel ever, which became a bestseller become a movie!"

"Really? That's great Michelle! Congratulations! No wonder you were praising God the way you were. Can I have your autograph?"

Michelle started laughing.

"No, I'm serious. Here, write it on here, along with the name of your book. I have never met an author before! This is great!"

She did exactly that, bringing a big smile to Kyle's face.

"Thanks Michelle! This is really cool! I will be looking for this book when I get home. Knowing mom or my sister, they have probably already bought it. They are not going to believe I met you!"

"Well, it was a pleasure meeting you too, Kyle. I will be keeping my ears and eyes open for your name too!"

When Michelle arrived, she rented a car and went straight to her publisher's office downtown. Michelle walked in to see her editor sitting alongside her publisher.

"Girl! Why didn't you call me and tell me the exciting news?" Sheila asked.

"Well, it looks like I didn't have to. You are already here. Fact is, you probably knew before I did!"

"Yes, I called her first Michelle. Sorry. But I figured as excited as you were, you'd probably forget to call Sheila, so I did for you. Hope you didn't mind?"

"Oh no, I thought about it on the plane, but I thought I'd call when I got here. I'm glad you did call her! Thanks! So, what's the next step, on making my book a movie?"

"We have contacted the actors you suggested to play the parts, but not all of them are willing to do it."

"How about the main characters? Did you get the good looking Irish actor Blake Jordan and Casandra Kelly?"

"Yes. Yes, we did. It was very hard to reach them, but, when we did, they were happy to do it."

"Oh my gosh! We actually get to meet Heavenly Blake Jordan! Oh my gosh! What a babe he is!"

"Okay, calm down Michelle. Don't hyperventilate! So when do we start actually making the movie?"

"First thing in the morning. We have to be on the set bright and early at 6 a.m., sharp! They want to go over the first few chapters, and then start rolling."

"I can't believe this is actually happening! Here, pinch me, Sheila, to see if I'm dreaming."

"Owe!"

"You told me to pinch you. I wanted to make sure you knew, YOU ARE NOT DREAMING. You are definitely awake, Michelle. This is the REAL THING!"

They all started laughing as they got up to leave. Sheila offered Michelle to stay with her at her apartment again, which Michelle agreed. They got a bite to eat at a nearby café, before returning to the apartment. It was 7:30 p.m. She called her mom, to let her know she arrived and to let her know they were starting in the morning to make her movie. Her mom was as excited as she was and wished she could be there with her.

"Maybe before we're finished mom, I'll fly you and dad here, okay?"

"Oh Michelle, I'd absolutely love that! I love you honey. Be careful. Call me soon and let me know how it's going, okay? Oh, and give Blake a big kiss for me too!"

"Okay mom, like that will ever happen! Has Jesse called?"

"Yes, but I didn't tell him anything."

"I bet that went over like a lead balloon, huh?"

"Well, he had to go and said he'd call back, but hasn't yet."

"Oh well, remember, please, don't tell him ANYTHING, okay?"

"I'll be sure and not tell him anything. I promise."

"Okay, mom, thanks. I love you and dad too. Talk to you soon. Bye."

Chapter Seventeen

ix o'clock rolled around pretty quick, considering Michelle hardly slept a wink, thinking about her big day. She rolled out of bed and heard Sheila in the kitchen.

"Good morning. Did I wake you?"

"No, I set the alarm. I hardly slept at all. Can you believe we get to meet Blake? Oh my Gosh!"

"He sounds really nice and I believe you couldn't have picked a better actor to do the hero."

"And I just love Casandra Kelly too. She seems like she'd be so down to Earth as well. I bet they will just bring your book to life."

"I know! I can hardly wait to meet them both!"

"I've already taken my shower Michelle. So you better get in there. Time is wasting. Oh, and I killed a black spider that was in the shower. That is the second one I've seen this week."

They arrived on the set right on time. The producers were ready and waiting to meet Michelle as they came up to her and shook her hand, introducing themselves. Then they started going over her book, making notes and adjustments. They covered the first few chapters all morning, making a few changes, deleting and adding what they saw fit to, with Michelle's approval.

Michelle kept looking around, waiting for Blake and Michelle to show up.

"Michelle, who do you keep looking for?" one of the producers asked her.

"Oh, she's looking for Blake Jordan, aren't you Michelle?" Sheila teased her.

"And Michelle too, of course. They are still going to star in my book, aren't they?"

"Oh, the actors don't come on set until after we have gone over all the manuscript and made our adjustments, and made into script form. And we will be at this for at least another 5 hours. In fact, we may not get finished until tomorrow. Then we have to make it into script form, so the actors can read over and learn their lines. But don't you worry your pretty self about it. We'll get her done. Now, let's take a 45 and break for lunch."

Michelle was disappointed, but kept working with them diligently. After hearing Blake wasn't going to be showing up, she settled down, and concentrated more easily, getting completely finished with the revisions that afternoon.

"Are you sure you are happy with the changes we made and added?"

"Yes, completely. Thank you, so much, for being patient with me, and so kind. Charlie, you are the best! Thank you, a million times over."

"Michelle you have been a trooper, and a delight to work with yourself. Thanks for putting up with me. I'll see you back bright and early again, in the morning. I'll just make these into a script and make copies for everyone and pass them out tonight. Okay, it's a rap for today. Go get some rest, and I'll see you in the morning."

"Thanks again, Charlie. Bye."

Michelle was beat. It was 6:12 p.m. Patty, Sheila, and Michelle all went to dinner, eating at a China Buffet before they went home. When they arrived the next morning, the actors started arriving as well. Michelle saw several arrive, but still, no Blake. Michelle started getting worried and asked Charlie where he was. Charlie was the main producer.

"Honey stop worrying your pretty little head so much. Remember that he doesn't come in until after the second chapter. Now, calm down. You will get to meet him and all the actors soon. Now, go get a Krispy Crème donut, drink your chocolate milk, and relax."

"Okay, I'm sorry. It's just I'm so excited and so overwhelmed with.. It's my first book, first movie, it's all so…"

"I know. IT's hard to really take it all in at once. You will be okay, once you see the figures you're going to make, with this movie. I believe it will be a huge hit!"

"You really think so?"

"Yes, I do."

"Charlie Diamond, you have a phone call on line 1."

He patted her back and made a thumbs up, running to get his phone call. As soon as he finished his call, he gathered all the actors around. He took his microphone and started speaking.

"Good morning to you all. There are plenty of coffee and donuts for everyone, so help yourself. For those of you who have worked with me before, we can only hope you will agree we do have fun, working long and hard. The movie we are about to make was written by none other than Michelle Mertz herself. Come out here, Michelle. I believe you all will enjoy working with her, and will enjoy the story as well. She herself picked some of you to act in her movie, and I'm sure the pleasure is all hers, but you really ought to give her a big round of applause and thank her for choosing you."

They all smiled and gave her a big round of applause, showing their appreciation, as Michelle also, gave them an applause too.

"I just want to thank you all for being here, and accepting this job, acting as my characters, bringing them to life, from my book. Thank you all, so very much, and I hope you will enjoy and have fun making this movie as I will, watching it being made. Thank you again, from the bottom of my heart, you all."

They all clapped again, as Michelle left the stage.

They were about to wrap up the second day, when low and behold, Blake Jordan comes through the doors strutting his hot sexy stuff, over to Charles.

"Oh my gosh! Sheila, there he is! Sheila! Look!"

"Mr. Blake Jordan himself. Man girl, you sure know how to pick your heroes, don't you!"

"Oh my gosh! Here he comes! How do I look?"

"You look just lovely, darling. Allow me to introduce myself. Hi, I'm Blake Jordan. And you, must be the beautiful, soon to be famous, Michelle Mertz."

Blake took her hand and kissed the back of it, as Michelle was awe struck, smiling and not able to speak.

"It is quite an honor, and my great pleasure to finally meet you."

He'd turn to Sheila then, shaking her hand.

"And you are?"

"Sheila Winters. I'm her Ed.. Ed.."

Michelle elbowed her in the side so she would spit out the word she had tangled up in her mouth. "Editor!"

She shot a look to Michelle, that wasn't at all, pleasing, as his cell phone rang. As he was talking on his cell, Michelle and Sheila were both in amazement, listening to his oh so sexy Irish accent.

"Sheila, I didn't mean to elbow you so hard. Oh, here he comes again."

"Where were we? Ah yes, meeting you nice, lovely ladies. It is a great pleasure meeting you both. Until tomorrow then, have a wonderful evening."

He took Michelle's hand and kissed the back of it again, and then shook Sheila's hand. Blake then strutted himself out the door.

They just watched him leave, and turned to each other, like school girls and screamed.

"Can you believe who we just met?"

"Blake Jordan!" they both said together, still acting like teenagers.

"I will never wash my hand again!"

"Girl, me either! He didn't kiss mine, but oh does he have the nicest soft hands I've ever felt! I can't believe we actually met the one and only, biggest hunk of all time! WOW!"

"I know! I know! Mm., and he kissed my hand twice!"

Michelle held her hand up to her cheek, laying her head down, daydreaming.

"Uh, Michelle, I'm not sure, but that looks like your fiancé over there talking to Charlie."

Sure enough, when Michelle looked, it was Jesse. All she could think about was how in the world did he know she was here? Maybe he didn't know she was there. Or maybe her mom told him. She didn't know but wasn't at all pleased with Jesse being there. Michelle wanted to surprise Jesse with her book being made into a movie. And now, she couldn't."

"Michelle he hasn't even looked this way. Maybe he doesn't even know you're here."

"I don't know. Why else would he be here? I believe he knows, but how? He must have sweet talked my mom into telling him. He has a way of getting information, and a way of getting it out of people too, and God only knows how he does it!"

"But aren't you at least bit delighted to see him?"

Michelle looked away from watching Jesse and looked at Sheila, with a little grin, shaking her head yes. Sheila knew Michelle was so in love with Jesse and couldn't wait to be his wife.

"I guess. But after meeting Blake Jordan, he better have a good reason why he is here! I'm just disappointed I couldn't surprise him."

Jesse walked up to Michelle, taking her into his arms and kissed her passionately.

"Hi, my beautiful love. I've missed you something fierce and just had to see you. I hope you don't mind. Hello, Sheila, how are you?"

"Fine Jesse, thanks. I'll leave you two alone. Michelle, I will see you back at the apartment, right?"

"Ugh, yea, okay Sheila. I'll see you later."

Jesse learned towards Michelle again to kiss her, but Michelle pulled back from him.

"Just how did you know I was here, Mr. Jesse Lee Fox? Tell me how. Did you sweet talk my mom Into telling you? Start talking right now."

"Michelle, don't get upset with me, or your mom. I…"

"So you did get it out of my mom! I knew I shouldn't have told her and leave without telling her where or what I was doing. But I didn't want her to worry about me and cause her to…"

"Oh so you don't want her to worry, but what about me? It's okay for me to worry, huh? You're soon to be husband. Thanks a lot."

Michelle, still looking at him, watching him get a little annoyed with her.

"Oh, Don't you EVEN go there with me Jesse! You didn't tell me WHERE or WHAT, you were doing when you left me! And I'm going to be your soon to be wife!"

Michelle, still looking at him couldn't help but laugh out loud, seeing his expression as he was imitating her. She hit him on his arm with a little force.

"Come here, you."

Jesse gently grabbed her, taking her into his loving arms, and kissed her deeply, causing her to get weak in the knees again, sick to her stomach, and lose her balance.

Jesse pulled away from her lips while catching her fall.

"Michelle, love, are you alright? You look white as a sheet. Come sit down here."

Jesse walked her over to the chair and helped her sit down, kneeling down beside her.

"Jess, please, pray for me..."

Michelle couldn't pass the uneasy feeling in her stomach and vomited in front of Jesse.

Sheila went and brought her a wet cloth and a trash can in case she threw up again. Jesse took her hand and prayed for her silently, moving her hair out of her face. After a few short minutes, Michelle looked into Jesse's eyes.

"Thank you, for being here. I really am happy to see you. I'm sorry I got upset with you. I just wanted to tell you about myself, about my book being made into a movie. Thank you, for praying for me. I'm starting to feel better now. That must have been some prayer."

"Are you sure you are feeling better? Your color is starting to come back. I didn't know I'd have this kind of effect on you, or I wouldn't have come."

"So, why are you here Jesse? You never did explain yourself."

They both heard familiar voices and looked up to see who they were. It was Casandra Kelly and Blake Jordan, rehearsing their lines.

Michelle let out a sigh of admiration, watching them rehearse. Most of the other actors had left and Charlie was about to leave too.

"Oh, so it wasn't me who had such an effect on you. I see who it was."

Michelle started laughing.

"Jesse, stop it. You are my one and only one who has that kind of effect on me; that I need and want for the rest of my life. Come on, let's get out of here. I'm ready to get a bite to eat, I think. I didn't eat much lunch."

As they were walking out, Blake caught a view of Jesse and waved at him. Michelle saw him wave, and thought he was waving at her, so she waved too, as Jesse did. Jesse started teasing Michelle again, about Blake having an effect on her. They got into Jesse's car and drove off to a quiet little Mexican Café, on Michelle's request. After they were seated, and had ordered, Jesse started explaining to Michelle.

"Michelle, I want and need to tell you why I am here."

"It's about time."

The waitress brought their drinks.

"When I couldn't reach you, I called your work and asked for Sandy, but she wouldn't tell me anything, except that you were okay, and not to worry. I then called Dawn, but she told me the same thing."

Michelle started laughing.

"See, see how it feels, when you are left in the dark, honey. It's not very fun now is it?"

Jesse gave her that ornery, warning look, and then continued his story. "So, that's when I called your mom and talked to her, but all she'd tell me is that you were out of town, and that it pertained to your book."

"Oh, really? So, mom didn't spill the beans then. Wow! I'm impressed! So, just how did you find out where I was?"

"Well, remember when I left and I promised you I'd tell you where I was and what I was doing?"

"Yes, and you promised no more secrets, that you'd tell me everything. Oh yes, I remember. So, tell me already."

Jesse started laughing as the waitress brought their orders and refilled their iced teas.

"Can I get you anything else?"

"No thanks."

"Okay, my name is Julie if you change your minds."

"Thank you Julie."

Jesse took Michelle's hand and he'd pray over their food.

Jesse took a bite of his chicken enchilada, and looked at Michelle.

Michelle anxiously waited for him to finish his story.

"Jesse! Please tell me already. You know how much I hate suspense!"

She said it a little loud, and people looked over at them. Jesse started laughing, just aging her on.

"Shhh, okay, okay. Calm down. Are you ready?"

"Jess… I'm warning you."

"I have written a book too, well, several actually, but this particular one, has been published and was made into a movie as well."

"Nuh uh! No way!"

Jesse was laughing, loving her reaction.

"I'm serious, Love. And believe it or not, Broznan just finished acting in it. We finished filming it a couple days ago."

"No way! Get out of here! Are you serious Jesse?"

Jesse was laughing again.

"Yes, Michelle. I am serious as a heart attack. He played my private investigator."

"Wow! I am amazed! I am very impressed and very proud of you too. Oh Jesse. I can't believe it. This is most definitely a big surprise! You really have blown me away. But this still doesn't answer my question how you knew I was here."

"Well, Blake came over to me and introduced himself."

"He did the same to me and Sheila today. He even kissed my hand twice."

"Oh, he did, did he?"

"Mmmmmm."

111

"Well, we'll have to see about that. We started talking. I told him all about you and your book, telling him it may possibly be made into a movie. He asked me what book it was and I told him. That's when he told me he had been scheduled to be on your set this week. And that was 6 months ago. Blake is really a nice guy. We had a great time, shooting the movie, and been pretty good buddies ever since."

"Wow! That is awesome! This is all so cool, Jess!"

Michelle began eating her taco salad. And Jesse was finishing his meal.

"So, is it Blake who spilled the beans and spoiled my surprise for you? You even knew that my book was going to be made into a movie, before I did! I can't believe you didn't tell me. And all those times you called me, you didn't say anything!"

Michelle looked up at Jesse, shaking her head in disbelief.

"Remember when I first had called you and I cut the call short? That's when Blake introduced himself to me. Right before I called you. I really wanted to tell you then, but I wasn't ready to tell you yet."

"Oh, you weren't 'ready' to tell me yet," Michelle said sarcastically, while Jesse gave her that ornery warning look again.

"Blake must do that to all the authors of books, or whatever. He only shook Sheila's hand, but kissed mine. I thought it odd that he said it was a pleasure to 'finally' meet me. Jesse, this is so thrilling! Praise God! This is so GREAT! Glory to God!"

Laughing out loud, people were looking at them again.

"We better go before they throw us out of here."

"Yeah, we better. I'm too excited to eat anyway!"

"How are you feeling babe? You sure you are finished eating?"

"Darling, I couldn't be any better, than I feel right now. I'm overwhelmed with pure D Joy. My cup runneth over."

"When God blesses, HE really blesses, doesn't He?"

Leaving more than enough money for their dinner and tip, they got up and left. Jesse opened the door for her, as he always did, and then got into his side. They weren't quite ready to go their separate ways yet, so Jesse kept driving.

"Where are we going Jesse?"

"Blake had told me about a secret place, very few people I know about. It is a quiet place, with a beautiful view, he said."

As Jesse kept driving down the highway, Michelle slid next to him, caressing his leg, signing to the radio.

"Mmmmmm, that feels good. You don't know how much I've missed you Michelle."

Michelle just smiled at him, and continued to caress his leg and sing until the song was over.

"That makes two of us. I've missed you so very much, Jess. These past few months have been so long and drawn out without you. But I kept myself busy and made more progress on our wedding, and wedding vows."

"Oh? I thought we agreed on the ones we picked out together?"

"Mmmmmm, I thought so too, until God kept nudging me to some scripture to write down and kept pressing me to use as my wedding vows to you."

He pulled onto a road off the highway, and followed it for about a mile, until he came to a beautiful park, with lots of trees and a few picnic tables. There was a couple of swing sets, a teeter totter, a merry-go round, and a large slide. He kept driving a bit longer, and stopped the car in front of a pretty look off point, that looked over a huge lake.

Jesse turned to face Michelle and looked into her eyes.

"I truly love you, Michelle Renee' Mertz."

He kissed her passionately.

"Mmmmmm, and you taste so good too."

"Oh, do I now? What do I taste like?"

"I'm not quite sure. Let me see…"

He kissed her again, pulling her closer, caressing her back slowly. They stayed in each other's arms for quite a while, talking and listening to a CD of love songs that he had put in when he stopped the car. Michelle had laid her head against his chest at some point and had fallen asleep.

Jesse was in the middle of telling her a story from his childhood.

"And what do you think I said?"

When Michelle didn't answer him, he looked down at her, sleeping peacefully. So Jesse laid his head on hers, and drifted off to sleep too. It was early morning before Michelle woke up, still curled up next to Jesse. She looked at her watch and saw that it was 3:33 a.m. She looked up at Jesse and found him asleep. Smiling, she started rubbing her hand over his chest, after unbuttoning his shirt halfway, for a little more easy access. She couldn't resist it much longer, she thought, and was extremely delighted that it was less than four weeks till the wedding.

Since Jesse didn't respond to her touch, she continued, kissing him softly, as her fingers glided over his bare chest, over his nipples. This time, Jesse shifted, facing her more, but didn't open his eyes. She grinned, and watched him for a second or two. When he didn't waken, she continued kissing him. Taking his hand, she kissed the inside of his palm, then kissed his neck, moving up to his ear lobe, and kissed it. She'd look at Jesse again, and kiss his lips once, moving her hand slowly, caressing his thigh, getting closer to her destination. Once she reached her destination, caressing still, she kissed him again, wanting him to wake up.

This time, he woke up, looking at her with passion, and let her kiss him, more fully. He opened his mouth more, as she plunged her tongue in, and caressing her inner thigh urgently. Jesse cupped her face gently, as they both echoed into each other's mouth. After a few seconds, Jesse pulled away after a brief moment.

"I don't know if I can do this much longer without giving in Michelle. Let's just elope and run to Vegas tonight."

Looking at him, she knew exactly how he felt, because she felt the same way. Knowing their desires for one another were the same, getting much stronger and harder to break away from.

He began kissing her deeply, moving his hand down to her inner thigh and started caressing her passionately. She fell back onto the seat with ease, as he followed her. He whispered something into her ear, before taking her earlobe into his mouth. He continues to massage her, making her moan softly.

"Jesse, mm, please…"

"Jesse, mm, please what, my love?.."

Michelle tried to reach him, to caress him again, as he looked into her eyes. Jesse moved a little so she could touch what she wanted. When she reached him, she started caressing him again, undoing his pants.

Jesse leaned his head back, enjoying her touch, when the sudden ring of his phone stopped them both.

He'd sigh, looking at her. He reached for his phone, not looking at the bright screen to see who was calling, and pressed the ignore button.

"Jess, I want to continue on, and I am guiltier than you, for letting this go on as far as it did. I feel like I need to apologize to you, and we both need to ask for forgiveness from God, for sure."

Jesse smiled and shook his head. He took her hand into his, and he began to pray. He prayed a heartwarming prayer that brought tears to Michelle's eyes. Before he finished praying, Michelle opened her eyes and looked at Jesse. He even had a tear or two, strolling down his cheek. When he finished, he started the car and they drove back to the apartment.

"I bet Sheila thinks I kidnapped you or something."

Sheila can think what she wants, and she will. But we confessed our wrong doing to our Heavenly Father, and asked forgiveness, and repented. And that's all that matters. It's not anyone else's business. God and us, have everything under control."

Jesse laughed, but agreed with Michelle as he walked her up to the door.

"You look so tired hon. I'm sorry I fell asleep, and getting you back so late."

"Do I really look that bad? I think I fell asleep first, so what else could you have done, besides fall asleep too. Hey, you were telling me about your dog or something, before I fell asleep. It wasn't that you were boring or anything."

"Uh huh. We will see if I ever tell you a story again", teasing her.

"Jess! But isn't that why stories are told, to help people fall asleep?"

Jesse laughed out loud.

"Get some sleep, my love, and I will call you later. I love you Michelle, so much. More than you can ever dream possible."

"I love you too. Maybe they won't mind if I took off today. It's Friday. Besides, they know how I was sick and all."

"Maybe they won't mind. I'll call you later, Sweetheart. Get some rest now."

"Yes, my Darlin, I will. You too, get some rest. But I won't sleep near as well as I did earlier with you by my side."

"That makes two of us, my Love, but we can go to sleep, and have wonderful dreams of each other, right?"

"I guess, but it's just not the same, Jess. I love you so much, I can hardly bear being away from you."

"Let's see."

Jesse, being his ornery self, leaned back away from her, at arm's length, but still holding her hands. Michelle stepped back into his arms, as Jesse kept moving away from her, teasing and laughing all the while.

Michelle cornered him and hit him on his chest.

"Jesse! That wasn't very funny!"

He'd still be laughing his hearty laugh, she loved so much, as he hugged her tightly.

"I'm sorry baby. I'm sorry. Just you don't forget that you can't hardly bear staying away from me when you really get mad at me, okay?"

"Why? Are you saying you're guilty of something that I might get mad at you for?"

"No, not anymore, but I'm talking about in the future, the rest of our lives together."

"Well, let's see now. Let's turn the tables here, Honey. Can you bear being away from me?"

Playfully mocking Jesse, she leaned away from him at arm's length. Jesse gave her a daring look, pulling her closer to him, as Michelle tried to refrain, but failed.

"Come here, you! No, I can't bear being away from you either, and yes, I will remember this when you make me mad or attempt to make me mad, you silly goose."

"Well, Darlin, I hope we don't EVER let the sun go down on our wrath, and can openly talk about whatever is on our minds, avoiding getting mad all together."

"Oh, but if we don't have any disagreements, then we can't make up. And it's so much FUN, making out, I mean, making up."

"Disagreements are not fighting, therefore, how we can make "out", or make up, if we don't EVER fight?"

"My point exactly!"

Michelle just shook her head, looking at him, rolling her eyes and smiled.

"I better let you go in now, or Sheila will be up before you even go to bed."

"I know. I think I'm delirious, because everything I say doesn't seem to make sense anymore."

Jesse kissed her one last time, before letting her go in. She watched him go to the elevator. As he looked back at her, blowing her a kiss goodnight and winking, he held up his thumb, pinky, and pointer finger as to say I love you. Michelle flashed a sleepy smile and pointed to herself; crossed her arms in front of her chest, pointed to him, and blew a kiss as well to say I love you too. When she went inside, Michelle was trying to be very quiet as to not wake Sheila. She undressed, put her nightshirt on, brushed her teeth, and went to bed. By the time she got in bed, it was 4:30 a.m. It felt as though she had just fallen asleep when Sheila came in about 5:30, turning on her light to wake her up.

"Hey, girl! Rise and shine, like the sunshine! It's time to get up."

Michelle rolled over and looked at her, with a scowl on her face.

"What time is it? I just got to sleeping good and started dreaming."

"Just got to sleep? What time did you come in girlfriend? I went to bed around 9 last night and you weren't home then."

Michelle chuckled.

"No I wasn't, 'mom'. Please turn off the light? I'm really tired. Please let me sleep in today and not go in. Do you think they would understand if I took the day off?"

Sheila looked at her with questioning eyes.

"Maybe, if they knew why you're taking the day off. Let's hear it. I'm a little curious as to why you want to take the day off as well, so spill it sister."

Michelle started laughing, and proceeded to tell her just partly why she wanted to take the day off.

"So, olé' Jesse had a few secrets he shared with you, big ones at that! Not too shabby, both of you landing best sellers and movies! Congratulations! So you two were out celebrating into the wee hours then, huh?

"Yeah, you could say that. Plus, catching up on some things and talking about our wedding too."

"If Jesse is right with Mr. Blake Jordan and the producers, then you don't have anything to worry about. Shoot girlfriends, I envy you. But I am also very proud of you both. Roll over and go back to sleep. You don't have a care in the world. But I have only one more question."

"What?"

"What time did you get in?"

"Four."

"Four! What kept you out that late?"

"That's two questions, 'mom'."

"Okay, I deserved that. But I still want to know. Inquiring minds want to know."

Michelle started laughing at her again, throwing her pillow at her.

"If you shut my light off, I will tell you."

Sheila shut her light off, throwing her pillow back at her.

"Blake had told Jesse about a real neat quiet hideaway that hardly anyone knows about. That's where Jesse took me. We were there all evening just enjoying being together after so long apart. Then we both fell asleep in his car."

"Yeah, I bet you did!"

Sheila remarked, not believing she told the whole truth, walking out of Michelle's room. Michelle knew Sheila didn't believe her, but Michelle didn't care. That was only between God, her, and Jesse. That's all that mattered.

Chapter Eighteen

*I*t was 12:30 p.m., when Michelle was awakened by Sheila's answering machine. After her voice she heard Jesse's.

"Hey, my beautiful sleepyhead, are you…"

Michelle picked up the phone, beside her bed.

"Hey, Good-looking. Yes, I'm awake, barely. What time is it?"

"It's 12:32. I tried to call your cell phone, but I guess you didn't hear it. But I left you a message. The day is waiting, my love. I've been up, showered, and been out and about already. I bought us some breakfast."

"Mm, sounds good. How sweet of you. What is it?"

"Oh, some chocolate milk and banana nut muffins."

"Mm, that does sound wonderful my Darlin. I think I hear Sheila coming in for lunch. Hang on, babe."

"Sheila, is that you?"

There was no response.

"Sheila, 'mom, are you checking up on me again?"

"Jesse, someone is here and it's not Sheila I don't think."

"Maybe it's the cleaning lady."

"Uh Sheila, if that's you, you better answer me right now!"

"Jesse, they are coming closer to my bedroom, Jesse!", Michelle whispered into the phone.

Michelle was getting scared. The phone went dead, and she wondered if someone had cut the line. Michelle let out a blood curdling scream. Suddenly, Sheila burst out laughing, coming towards her bedroom. Michelle looked up towards the doorway seeing Jesse poking his head in with Sheila hiding behind him.

"YOU GUYS ARE NOT FUNNY ONE LITTLE BIT!"

"Do you see me laughing, my love? Here, let me feed you breakfast in bed Darlin. Maybe that will help that growling tiger."

"Is it safe to come in?"

Jesse held up the bag of hot muffins and her chocolate milk in front of his face, peeking around the bag, looking at her, grinning. Michelle swung her pillow at him in the air, shaking her head, smiling. Jesse always knew how to make her smile that beautiful smile he loved about her.

"You know very well I cannot stay mad at you for very long Jesse Lee Fox. And yes, I demand you to feed me every bite of breakfast."

Jesse sat beside her on the bed, nuzzling her neck, kissing her.

"Oh, you demand me to feed you breakfast now, huh? What if I decide not to? What then?"

He started tickling her.

"Is that all you want me around for is to feed you all the time?"

Michelle was laughing so hard and hitting him to stop tickling her.

"Jesse! Stop! You are going to make me pee! Jess! I'm warning you!"

Jesse was laughing too but stopped as she demanded.

Sheila stepped into the bedroom as she was laughing at both of them.

"I'm sorry Michelle. It was my idea to scare you. Will you ever forgive me, please?"

"I don't know. I will have to think about that.", as Michelle looked at Sheila with an honoree grin.

"Oh Blake told me to tell you that he missed your pretty face today on the set and to give you this."

Sheila handed her a big beautiful pink rose in a pretty glass etched vase.

"Oh, it's very pretty! Mm, it smells divine as well! Ok, you are forgiven, with one exception. That you don't EVER scare me like that again. Look honey, what Blake gave me. Are you jealous?"

Michelle was laughing again.

"No because I was the one who picked it out for you when he and I went to lunch."

"Oh so that's why you're not jealous, huh? What if he picked it out on his own and gave it to me? Would you have been jealous then?"

"No."

Michelle laughed out loud again, rolling over to the other side of the bed to go to the restroom.

"Hey Ms. Orneriness. What if Casandra Kelly gave me a...rose? Would you... be jealous?"

"Not if I could pick it out for you I."

"So you are saying you'd be if she gave me a rose on her own without you knowing?"

"OMG! You two are totally pathetic! Sheila laughed as she walked out of the room.

Michelle came out of the restroom and crawled back into bed beside Jesse, covering up. Jesse handed her the chocolate milk he opened for her, along with a hot banana muffin. Jesse teased her, bringing the muffin to her mouth to take a bite, and then pull it away.

"Jesse!"

"I want to kiss you first, and then I want you to answer my question."

Michelle would begin kissing him the way she knew he loved, answering him, reassuring him with her love.

"Did I answer your question, good lookin?"

"No.", he continued teasing her.

"Oh whatever. No I wouldn't be jealous if she gave you a rose without me knowing."

Jesse laughed out loud.

"Oh "whatever!"

Jesse loved imitating her at times, teasing her, making her laugh. He loved her laugh, her smile and everything about this lovely lady. Michelle took a drink of her chocolate milk and sat it on the night stand by the rose. Jesse gave Michelle a bite then of the muffin first, and then he took a bite. Sheila came back into the room.

Oh, I almost forgot to tell you. I have a date with Charlie after the shoot today. It may be a late night, so don't wait up, okay?"

"Okay, have a nice time. Don't do anything I wouldn't do."

Sheila started laughing.

"Yea, okay."

Sheila left the room again, leaving out the front door and locking it as she closed the door.

As they finished eating the muffin, Jesse stood up and went to the restroom, then return. He was rubbing his lower back as if it was hurting.

"What's wrong with your back babe?"

"Oh, it's nothing. I woke up with it a little stiff and sore this morning, for some reason."

He sat back down on the bed and lay down beside Michelle, as she started rubbing her hands over his back.

"Mm, your hands feel good."

"My poor baby. Have you taken anything for it?"

"Yea, it's getting better. I believe you are making it feel better with your special loving touch."

"I will take care of you now and forever. I love you so very much Jess. Please don't ever leave me again, ever. I missed you something terrible."

"Baby, I just went to the bathroom."

"Jesse! You know what I'm talking about."

He started laughing, turning onto his side to face her

"Yes, my precious beautiful love, I do. I love you too, more than I could ever begin to show you. I promise I will never leave you again, like I have in the past few months."

They'd kiss passionately, as Michelle's hands roamed up and down his back and then moving towards his front side. Jesse stopped her hand before it reached its destination.

"Michelle love, we best not get caught up in…"

Michelle stopped his words by kissing him again and continued to reach her destination, rubbing slowly up and down. She pulled away from her kiss.

"Jesse, please. It will be okay. Relax. We are getting married. Besides, we won't do anything that we will be ashamed of and couldn't tell our granddaughter about."

Jesse grinned, thinking about Barbie and noticing Michelle called her our granddaughter, which thrilled him. Michelle lay her head on his shoulder then, snuggling closer as she continued her journey.

Michelle slipped out of bed quietly, being careful not to wake Jesse. She took a shower and got ready for the fun filled day they had discussed earlier, going to Universal Studios.

When Michelle came out of the bathroom, Jesse was on the phone, talking to Barbie.

"Yes honey, she's fine. In fact, here she is now."

Jesse handed his phone to Michelle.

"Hi Barb. How are you doing?"

Jesse got up and kissed Michelle and then went to the restroom. Minutes later, Michelle heard the shower go on as she was finishing up her conversation with Barbie.

"Okay babe, see you then. Be careful. I love you too. Ok, I will. Bye-bye."

Jesse came out of the bathroom.

"Barbie told me to tell you that she loves you and that her and your daughter will be shopping for our wedding this weekend. She's such a sweet girl. She must take after her sexy grandpa."

Jesse kissed the top of her forehead, smiling.

"Mmmmmm, you always smell so wonderful Jesse."

"Thank you. You do too, as a matter of fact."

"Why thank you kind sir."

"So is your daughter and son accepting our marriage now?"

"Yes. I think they were just shocked in the beginning. But they know how I feel about you and have always felt since I met you. And after they meet you, they will see why I'm so crazy about you."

"Awe…."

"How's your parents and siblings? And Dawn?"

"Oh they are all fine for the most part. But they would love to be here with us, to watch my book come to life. Especially mom and Dawn."

"Why don't I fly them all down so they can?"

"No, you don't have to do that. That would be so expensive babe. Besides we are just getting started. I'd love for them to meet all the cast members though, especially Blake."

Michelle couldn't keep a straight face, watching Jesse when she mentioned Blake Jordan and was laughing out loud.

"Especially Blake, huh? What about Casandra Kelly?"

"I said all the cast members."

Michelle started laughing again.

"Just what am I going to do with you?"

"God only knows but I know what I am going to do with you."

Michelle started sliding his shirt off his shoulders and started kissing his chest, stopping at one of her favorite spots, caressing his nipple. She winked at him and then Jesse walked her backwards until she fell back onto the bed and took possession of her lips. Jesse's hands roamed down her freshly shaven soft smooth tanned legs slowly. He was kissing her with burning desire as his long fingers caressed her, brushing lightly along and around her satin bikini underwear. Michelle arched up to him with sizzling desire, pleading to him to do more. He'd kiss her again as he slipped his hand inside, caressing slowly, moving his fingers ever so loving, fulfilling her desire once again.

Moments later, they were in each other's arms.

"We better finish getting ready and leave for Universal Studios."

"Yea, I guess we better. I'm looking forward to it."

"Me too!"

Michelle rolled to the other side of the bed, went to blow dry her hair, curl it and put her makeup on. Jesse got up to, picking up his shirt off the floor and went into the kitchen to pour himself some OJ. He picked up a newspaper off the coffee table in the living room before he sat down on the sofa. As Jesse sat down, something bit him on his hand, making it sting. Jesse looked around and saw a spider crawling away. He took a magazine from the table and smacked the spider until it was dead. Jesse went back into the kitchen to find a paper cup to scoop the spider in. He had remembered reading if at all possible, to capture the insect if ever bitten by one, and bring it with you to the ER. After he scooped the spider into the paper cup, he washed his hands thoroughly. He noticed there were two faint red spots with redness around them and his hand was swelling. In the meantime, Michelle finished getting ready and walked out of the bedroom to find Jesse slouched over on the sofa, white as a sheet. She ran over to him and saw his right hand really red and swollen up like a balloon.

"Oh Jesse! What happened baby?"

Jesse was out of breath, trying to tell her what happened, but pointed to the cup on the coffee table. She looked in the cup.

"Oh Jesse! Hang in there Baby!"

Michelle helped him to the car and caring the cup that the spider was in, making sure it stayed in the cup.

"Thank God, Sheila lives next door to the hospital! Thank You Jesus! Oh God, in Jesus name, please touch Jesse right now. Don't let anything happen to him please precious Jesus. Thank You for hearing and answering my prayers in advance. Amen."

In seconds, they were in front of the ER doors. Michelle got out and rushed around to Jesse's door, hollering for someone to help them. A couple Paramedics came right over with a stretcher and hooked Jesse up with oxygen and I.V.

He got bitten by this spider a few minutes ago. Thank you gentlemen. I'll be right there Jesse! I'm going to park the car and I will be right in. Hang in there baby!"

"He will be in room 3 ma'am."

"Ok, thanks again."

Michelle moved the car to the nearest parking space and ran into the ER looking frantically for room three. A kind lady at the front desk got Michelle's attention.

"Ma'am, are you with the gentleman the Paramedics brought in just now?"

"Yes, yes I am. Oh, I bet you need some information to get him checked in. I'm sorry. Here is his driver's license and insurance card."

"Thank you."

The lady typed the information she needed and handed back Jesse's driver's license and insurance card back to Michelle.

"Ok, you can go thru this door when it opens. Room three will be to your left."

"Thank you."

The door opened and Michelle was in room three and at Jesse's side within seconds. Jesse was having some kind of spasm attack as the nurse was administering something into his IV.

"Oh my God! You are killing him! What are you doing!? Stop!"

"Ms. We are doing everything we can to help him. Are you his wife?"

"I hope to be! We are engaged. What are you giving him?"

Michelle was streaming tears, praying in the Holy Ghost underneath her breath, watching Jesse. She had never seen him look so pitiful and in distress before and it scared her. She happened to remember him giving her a list of his medications and what he was allergic to as she rummaged through her purse and finally found it.

"This is Penicillin. It will help counteract the poison from the spider."

"He is highly allergic to Penicillin! Here is a list of his medications and what he is allergic to."

The nurse stopped immediately the IV injection and fumbled around to take the IV out of his arm and to put a brand new one in. She took the contaminated bag down from the hook and left the room. Michelle didn't take her eyes off Jesse, still praying for him. She heard them say outside the door that it was a Black Widow spider, and that it could cause convulsions. Michelle was still crying but believed

God was with him and was going to heal him. Jesse flatlined just then and the nurse and a doctor came flying in telling Michelle to get out.

"CODE BLUE! CODE BLUE!"

More doctors came rushing in with paddles.

"Ms. In sorry, but you need to step out please. We are doing everything we can."

Chapter Nineteen

Michelle hesitantly stepped out but sat right outside the door, listening to every word they were saying from his room, still praying earnestly. After it seemed like an eternity passed, the nurse opened the door. Michelle jumps up and looked into the room, thankfully finding Jesse still alive.

"Honey, he will be okay. We had to resuscitate him trice though. We gave him a new IV bag to help flush out the Penicillin completely and then gave him anti-venom shot, a pain killer and muscle relaxer to start off with. He will be pretty sore for a while but he will be okay. He will be staying overnight or two for observation though. Don't worry. We will be getting him into a room upstairs as fast as we can."

"Thank you. Can I go in now?"

"Yes, he's been asking for you, Michelle is it?"

"Yes".

"My name is Ms. Ogle. Don't hesitate to call for me if and when you need anything. Okay?"

"Okay, thank you Ms. Ogle."

As Michelle walked into the room and walked up beside him, she started to cry again. Jesse looked so helpless. Jesse tried to reach up and wipe away her tears but didn't have any strength. He just shook his head slowly and touched her hand, giving it a weak loving squeeze. Jesse still had his oxygen mask on and couldn't talk, but was getting restless like he was looking for something.

"Honey, what is it? Point Baby, point."

Jesse pointed to the trash can. As soon as Michelle lifted it up to him, he bent over it and Michelle lifted his oxygen mask off just in time before he threw up.

"Ms. Ogle, Ms. Ogle! He's throwing up!"

Ms. Ogle and a doctor came rushing in a few seconds later to see what was wrong. Jesse was still throwing up as Michelle was still holding the trash can for him. Jesse leaned back onto the bed he was on for a few seconds, and then started throwing up again, shivering. The doctor looked at his chart and over the lists Michelle had given them earlier.

"Doctor, is this part of the reaction from the bite or the medicine?"

Ms. Ogle exited the room.

"A combination of both, I'm afraid. I will be giving him something for his upset stomach and something to help him sleep peacefully. This should stop his vomiting and help ease him into relaxation."

The doctor exited the room, giving orders to Ms. Ogle as she entered the room with a warm blanket she had heated up for Jesse. She had put it over him as Jesse leaned back onto the bed. The nurse also gave him a wet cloth to use and then stepped out of the room again. After she had returned, she administered the medicine the doctor ordered for him, into his IV. It was a few minutes and Jesse stopped vomiting. Ms. Ogle was monitoring him awhile before she left the room, putting his oxygen back on him and replacing the mask to the nose tubes.

"They have his room ready upstairs I was told and they have someone on their way to come get him. He will be in room 712."

"Ok, thank you again, so much Ms. Ogle. You have been most helpful. May God bless you."

"Thank you, and you two may God bless you on your upcoming wedding."

"Thank you."

When they came and took Jesse to his room, Michelle followed them as she called Barbie.

"Barbie, this is Michelle. Honey, your grandpa was bitten by a Black Widow Spider, but he's going to be fine now. We are in the Los Angeles Memorial hospital. He has to stay here a day or two, to make sure…"

"They didn't give him Penicillin, did they?"

"Barbie, yes, but quickly removed it and gave him other drugs to help counteract it. They are taking him to his room as we speak. He will be in room 712."

"Thank you Michelle for calling me. Mom and I will catch the next flight out. Please tell him I love him and that we are on our way. You hang in there too Michelle. Be tough for grandpa. When he sees you being strong, it helps him be strong. I love you too Michelle. See you soon."

"Okay Barb, I love you too. Be careful. See you when you get here."

"Sweetheart, I'm right here. Barbie and your daughter are on the next flight to see you."

Jesse slowly nodded his head, blinking his eyes, to let her know he understood. He looked so tired Michelle thought. They arrived to his hospital room as they transported him onto the bed, making sure his IV was in place and that he was comfortable before they exited. Shortly after, the nurse came in, introduced herself, and then asked questions while she was taking his vitals. "Honey, do you want anything?"

Michelle poured a glass of ice water from the plastic pitcher that was sitting on the table in front of him and gave him a drink. She then kissed his forehead, telling him she loved him before she sat down in a chair beside him until he dozed off to sleep. It wasn't long until Jesse was fast asleep and seemed to be sleeping peacefully like the doctor informed her. Michelle slipped out and called Sheila to tell her what had happened.

"Sheila, it's Michelle. I'm sorry to bother you, but wanted to tell you we are in the hospital next to your apartment. Jesse got bitten by a Black Widow spider in your apartment this morning."

"Oh my gosh! Really? Is he alright? Where was he bitten?"

"In your living room, on his hand. Yes, he is doing better than he was. He is sleeping peacefully now. But he coded twice but thank God he pulled through. Plus they gave him Penicillin which he is highly allergic to. I was so scared Sheila."

"Oh my God Michelle. Is he going to be okay? How are you holding up? Do you need any company?"

"No, yea, he's going to be okay now I believe. I'll be okay. I called his granddaughter and her and her mom are probably on a flight right now on the way up here. That was about 30 minutes ago when I called them."

"Are you sure you don't want any company, just until they get there?"

"No. I'll be fine. Go on with your plans. I just felt like you needed to know and maybe you could tell them on the set what happened."

"Okay, I sure will. Hang in there Michelle. Jesse is pretty tough. He will be just fine. Call me though, if you need ANYTHING, alright? Promise me."

"Ok, I promise. Thank you Sheila."

Michelle peeked into Jesse's room to see if he was still asleep and he was. She walked down to the hospital dining room and called her parents and Dawn, to let them know what happened. They was sorry to hear about Jesse, but was so excited about both her and Jesse's books being made into movies. After Michelle made all of her phone calls, she went back up to Jesse's room to check on him again. His covers was pulled down which was a good sign his temperature had broken. He was still sleeping soundly, which she was glad. She looked at the clock on the wall, seeing it was 5:15 p.m. She pulled out the beef jerky out of her purse she had got out of the vending machine on the movie set the other day and a bag of chips. Michelle sat down in the chair beside Jesse, flipping through a magazine while eating. When she finished eating, she poured herself a glass of ice water, took a drink and then curled up and fell asleep in the chair.

Michelle woke up a couple hours later when she heard Barbie and her mom come walking into the room. When she opened her eyes, she noticed Jesse awake, sitting up and changing channels on the television.

"Hi grandpa. How are you feeling?"

"Hi daddy. It looks like you are feeling better."

They approached him giving him gentle hugs and kisses.

"Hello my lovelies. Yes, I'm doing and feeling better than earlier. But I am really sore and still weak. Michelle Love, meet my beautiful daughter, Stephanie. Stephanie, meet Michelle, my soon to be gorgeous better half."

"Hi Stephanie. It's a pleasure finally getting to meet you, although under poor circumstances. Hello Barbie. I'm so glad you girls were able to come."

"Yes, it's nice to finally meet you too Michelle. Are you sure you are ready to handle my daddy? He can be quite the handful."

"Here, here now. I totally resent that remark."

"You had quite a time this morning Babe. I felt so sorry for you and felt so helpless, but I kept praying, believing you was in God's hands. I thank God, HE, was with you all the way."

"Amen. Thank You Jesus, for taking care of me. And thank you my Darlin, for praying and being here with me."

"I wouldn't be anywhere else Jesse Lee Fox. I love you so much and I will take care of you no matter what, for the rest of our lives together."

"Well, that's sweet Michelle, and good to know. It looks like a miracle has taken place here, in all aspects." Stephanie said.

"Yes, now that I see your dad feeling and looking a lot better than this morning, it makes me very happy and very thankful. They had to resuscitate him twice because they gave him Penicillin which you know he is highly allergic to. So they counter acted that with something, plus exchanging his IV bag. And then he got sicker than a dog and threw up his insides. Bless is heart. He has been through a lot the past few hours. But after they brought him to the room, he finally got comfortable enough to fall asleep and seemed to be resting peacefully. At one point, he had pulled down his blankets, showing signs his temperature had broken, and that's when I fell asleep then too."

"Well you know what they say. You can't keep a good man down. Seriously, I believe God spared my life, and miraculously healed me. I give HIM, ALL the glory, honor and praise."

"That's great daddy. We do serve an Awesome Healing God."

Michelle, Barbie, and Jesse all said Amen.

"I do believe you have been an inspiration to my dad Michelle. I have been noticing a change in him, little by little, but all in a good way. Not that he was bad or anything. I want to thank you for being in his life and want to welcome you into our family."

Stephanie reached out and hugged Michelle as Michelle started to cry.

"Thank you Stephanie. You don't know how much that means to me to hear that from you."

"Well, Barbie has informed me on quite a lot, how you and dad get along together. It was meant to be it seems. I believe you have made a positive difference in dad. God knows someone needed to."

Stephanie looked at Jesse smiling, and then shot Michelle a wink.

"Hey, hey! What are you talking about?"

"See what I mean."

They started laughing as the nurse brought Jesse's dinner. It was only chicken broth, some Cherry Jell-O and vanilla ice-cream.

"Wow grandpa. That looks yummy, don't you think? Let me help you."

Barbie proceeded to help him, taking the lids off the food bowels. Jesse finished all but a small amount of his broth and a bite or two of his Jell-O and ice-cream, leaving it for Barbie to finish. They all visited until visiting hours were over at 9 p.m.

"Well grandpa, we better go so you can get a full night's rest and feel even better tomorrow. I love you so much. Get 100% because I want you to take us to Universal Studios."

"Yea daddy, we better go before they kick us out here. I love you. You sleep well, ok. We shall see you tomorrow."

"Ok. Thank you for coming, but you didn't have to. I love you too; I'm in very good hands, as you can tell."

"Yes, I can tell. Thank you again Michelle, for calling us, and taking care of this lovable man. Good night Michelle. See you in the morning daddy."

Barbie and Stephanie gave kisses and hugs good-bye and left to go to Jesse's hotel room that he insisted on them staying at.

The next day, Jesse was released from the hospital. Michelle drove him back to his hotel, helping him out of the car, walking with her arm around his waist to his hotel room. Barbie and Stephanie were shocked to see them so early as they were still in their nightgowns. Michelle and Jesse came walking in with a bag full of freshly baked blueberry and banana muffins.

"Mmmmmm…something sure smells delicious.", Stephanie said.

"Rise and Shine my beauties. How did I'll sleep?"

"Ugh…what time is it?" Barbie said sleeplly, rubbing her eyes.

"It is 8:07 a.m. Here, try Ruby's famous muffins. Banana or Blueberry?"

Jesse pulled out one of each and presented them to Barbie and Stephanie. He saw that the phone was blinking on the hotel phone, that he had a voice message.

"Hmm, I wonder who called me."

"I don't know, but I heard the phone ring around 6:30 this morning! Whoever it was, better have a very good reason why they called."

Jesse looked at the phone number and recognized the number, smiled and then laughed out loud. He couldn't wait to see the look on everyone's faces when they heard the voice that called and left a message.

"Let's see now, how do I retrieve this voice mail?"

Jesse found and pushed the button, putting it on speaker.

"Jess, you OLE dog! This is Blake. What's this I hear about a widow biting you? What have I told you about those widows? They are deadly mate. And not just the spiders either. Hahaha. Hey listen, take care of yourself. And give me a holler when you feel better."

That voice sounds familiar," Barbie said, looking at her mom, then at Jesse.

"Play that back again grandpa."

So Jesse plays it back, winking at Michelle, grinning.

"Michelle, do you know who it is?"

"Yea, but with the warning look your grandpa is giving me, I best not say. Sorry, you are on your own babe."

"Oh my gosh! Was that who I think it was?" Connie looked at Jesse.

"Daddy! How does HE know you!?"

Jesse started laughing.

"Okay guys, who is it?"

"Remember, Bound Jimmy Bound, 007," Jesse asked Barbie.

"OH MY GOD! You actually know Blake Jordan!? Grandpa! OH MY GOD! That was Blake Jordan on your answering machine!"

While Jesse and Michelle were laughing, Barbie and Connie were looking at each other in disbelief.

"Yes, yes it was," Jesse would do a poor imitation of his voice.

I told you guys last night that he starred in my book and played the private investigator. I don't know. It's still pretty amazing to me really. After him introducing himself to me, during the making of the movie, we just kind of hit it off. Been buddies ever since."

"WOW! Have you been to his house?"

"Only once. He had invited me over to fill in for one of his buddies for poker."

"Cool! I'd love to meet him grandpa! He is so HOT! SSS! Don't you think so too Michelle?"

"Uh yea! I mean, he's okay."

Michelle laughing looked at Jesse, giving her that threatening look.

"He is a lot more than okay Michelle, admit it! I will protect you from gramps."

"Okay Barbie, if you promise to protect me, then yes, he is very HOT! SSS!"

Michelle laughed, hiding behind Barbie, as they all laughed, with Barbie holding back Jesse from grabbing Michelle.

"But he couldn't EVER hold a candle to my Jesse."

She'd pause for a second or two.

"I don't think anyways."

Then Michelle took off running into his bedroom, shutting the door, collapsing onto his bed. When he came into the bedroom, he gently pinned her to the bed.

"What did you say now about you 'didn't think' Blake could ever or never hold a candle to me?"

He started tickling her until she was laughing so hard she was crying.

"Okay! You know you are my one and only, mighty hunk of a man, whom I will always and forever not only think but KNOW you're HOT! SSS! And NO ONE could ever hold any kind of candle to you. Never ever, nu-uh, no sir re!"

Jesse smiling, looked at her, and helped her wipe away her joyful tears, because she was laughing so hard.

"So your one and only what? Hunk of a mighty man you said?"

"Yes Darlin you are. Oh how I love you my one and only sexy, charming, hunk of a mighty man. My one true love. Now my lips have been aching, suffering from malnutrition from your warm, sexy kisses, so please would you rescue them?"

"You wish is my ever command, my beautiful, lovely, witty, love of my life."

Jesse gave her loving kisses and then they both went back out to join Barbie and Connie.

"Well, what should we do today girls?"

"Mom and I still need to go shopping for your wedding. Are you up for it Michelle?"

"Yeah that sounds good to me. Jess, do you feel like shopping with us girls?"

"Oh no, thanks but no thanks. I have been there and done that, and don't care to do that again. You go ahead though, have fun. I'm going to stay around here, catch up on my reading and call Blake back as well."

"That is still amazing dad, that you and Blake are friends."

"I agree grandpa! Hey maybe you could hook me up with him! We could have a double wedding and I could be the next Mrs. Blake Jordan!"

And they all laughed together, and then the girls left to go shopping while Jesse settled down to his book that he had been reading. After a couple of hours, Jesse made his call to Blake.

"Hey Blake. I'm returning your phone call. Thanks for calling. How's it going?"

"Hey bud, how are you feeling? I heard you had to stay the night in the hospital."

"Man, guess news travels fast around here. I'm fine. It's just a little ole bite. Guess I gave Michelle a scare though. Said they had to use the paddle on me twice to bring me around. I'm allergic to Penicillin, and they gave me some, which made me sicker than a dog, on top of all the other medicine they gave me. It was no picnic. Don't want to do it again, that's for sure. But I'm doing alright now other than being sore from the paddles and still a little weak."

"I'm sorry to hear you had such a rough go of it Jess. I told you those Black Widows can be deadly. But I'm glad you're doing better. How about you and Michelle come up for dinner tonight at my place? I will throw some prime rib on the ole Barbie."

Jesse began to laugh.

"It's really funny you mention that. See my granddaughter is named Barbie. Michelle had called her yesterday to tell her that I was in the hospital and she and my daughter were on the next flight out. They are here now. Well, actually, they all went wedding shopping. They both would love to meet you. They can't believe I am friends with you."

"Oh really? Well then, why don't we make a believer out of them. Ask them when they get back if they'd like to have dinner at my place tonight."

"But I think you should call back and ask them personally, buddy. I'm sure they all would be delighted. My granddaughter is wanting me to, how she put it, "hook her up" with you and plan a double wedding."

They both started laughing.

"Well, as much as I'd like to be your grandson-in-law, I'm afraid I will have to pass on that. I'm currently seeing another lovely lady, by the name of Julianna, which will also be joining us this evening."

They finished up their conversation and Blake agreed to call back, asking them personally to come have dinner at his house. Jesse continued his reading lying down on the bed. When the girls got back a couple hours later, they found Jesse asleep with his Bible across his chest.

"Now that is a Kodak moment. I've got to get a picture."

Barbie took her cell phone out and snapped a couple pictures, which woke him up.

"Oh hey girls. How was shopping?"

Michelle kissed him, sitting on the bed beside him.

"We had so much fun. We shopped until we dropped. How about you Barb, Stephanie?"

"Yes, we did too. We had a wonderful time together. Didn't buy a whole lot. Dad, do you remember that old picture we used to have, with Jesus ascending into Heaven?"

"Yea, I think so. What about it?"

"Whatever happened to it?"

"I believe your Aunt Judy has it, for some reason, if I remember correctly."

"Well, I found another one just like it today, in a beautiful frame, only it has the perfect poem on it too, that goes great with it. I bought it. I always loved that picture and the poem is a bonus!"

"That's great honey. Barb, what did you buy?"

"A couple of cute outfits, earrings, some cute sandals and perfume. Oh some new makeup and something for you and Michelle, my new "gramma"".

Barbie and Stephanie started laughing, looking at Michelle, watching her blush and laughing too.

"Girls please, stop it! I told you that makes me feel weird."

Michelle looked at Jesse, shaking her head, smiling.

"Well you did call her our granddaughter the other day. So what did you buy Love?"

"Oh a little of this and a little of that. Not too much."

"You ought to see what she bought for the honeymoon Grandpa!"

"Barbie! Shhh, that's a surprise!"

"Yea, he'll be surprised alright, "grandma `""".

They all laughed out loud as Jesse looked at the clock and saw that it was 4:47p.m. Blake should be calling anytime now, he thought and as Jesse got up to go to the restroom, he heard his cell phone ring.

"Would someone answer that please? I'm expecting a call."

"From who?" Barbie asked, looking around for his cell phone, which was lying on the bed. Barbie picked it up and it said Blake calling on the screen as it kept on ringing.

"Blake!"

Barbie answered the phone.

"Hello?"

"Hello. Might I be speaking with the lovely Barbie by chance?"

"Ughh…yea."

Barbie couldn't speak. Jesse came out of the bathroom, laughing.

"Hello? Are you still there?" Blake asked. Jesse took his phone from her and put him on speaker.

"Hi Blake. I'm putting you on speaker, since my granddaughter can't speak. What's up?"

"Is everyone there? You're lovely Michelle?"

"Hello Blake. How are you?" Michelle asked him.

"Great, thank you for asking. Is the lovely Stephanie there too?"

"Yes, yes I am."

"Fantastic! I am personally inviting you all to my place tonight for a swimming party and BBQ. Will you all please join me and my beautiful lady friend?"

Barbie, Stephanie and Michelle all looked at Jesse, with their mouths open in shock.

"Jess, are you still there buddy? What's happening?"

"Well, I believe they are all in shock. Girls, what do you say? Answer the gracious man, for Heaven's sake."

All three ladies answered in unison.

"YES WE WILL BE THERE!"

And then they all started giggling like school girls.

"Thank you Blake! Thank you so very much!", Michelle managed to speak out before Jesse took him off speaker and finished up their conversation.

"He said he was going to have Prime Rib on the Barbie, corn on the cob and shrimp shish kebabs."

"Wow! It sounds wonderful! Blake can eat Prime Rib or whatever else he wants on me anytime!"

They all started laughing as Stephanie scolded her daughter.

"So, what time did he say to be over?"

"He will send over his limo driver to pick us up around 6 p.m. he said."

"Oh my God! I can't believe Blake invited us to his house to eat dinner and swim! Blake! Blake Jordan! The hottest man alive!"

"It's true honey. Believe it. He is so nice and down to earth."

"It will be interesting to see how the rich and famous lives.", Stephanie said.

"Yes, it sure will. I need to figure out what to wear."

"No doubt! Oh man! What am I going to wear? I wasn't planning on wearing my new outfits this soon!"

"Ugh babe, I'd only wear one of them tonight, not both. Just saying."

Michelle teased her laughing.

"Oh you know what I meant, "grandma". What are you wearing?"

"Oh I'm not sure yet. Probably just jeans and a nice blouse, or something I bought for the honeymoon, teasing Jesse this time, looking at him with an honoree grin. Jesse looked at her with his daring eyes, barely smiling, giving her his warning look. Barbie looked at them, seeing their expressions. Barbie said, "You're in the doghouse now Michelle, and he hasn't even seen what it is yet. Green eyed…"

"Barbie Nicole, please shut the door on your way out, thank you." Barbie was familiar to his stern, firm voice and obeyed him.

"Jess, I was only teasing you, like you do me. You know I'd never do or say anything that intentionally hurt you. I love you. Come on now. I thought we went over this, like not too long ago."

Michelle tried to kiss him but he pulled back, still not softening his expression.

"Just what do you want me to do, to prove my love to you? And that I am in love with you, and ONLY YOU. Darlin, there is no other human being on God's green earth, that I'd rather be with, for the rest of my life. Jesse, you stole my heart years ago, right from the very beginning of time, I do believe. I simply cannot, and incapable of loving anyone else but you, and that is a fact Jack."

Jesse started smiling slowly and Michelle tried to kiss him again and succeeded this time but he pulled away quickly, looking at her.

"You are my only true love. You are my one and only hunk of a mighty, wonderful, Goodlookin sexy man throughout eternity."

This brought his heavenly smile back fully as he gently pushed Michelle back onto the bed, laying over her and began kissing her deeply. After a few minutes, she pulled away.

"Does that mean you have forgiven me?"

Jesse kissed her again, moving his hand to her bottom, pressing her closer to him so she could feel his desire underneath her.

"God, I want you Michelle…And yes, you are forgiven."

"Baby, as much as I want to make love to you right now, we best start getting ready."

Jesse started kissing her again with desire until they heard sacks rattling with Barbie opening the door.

"Didn't anyone teach you to knock first before entering?" Jesse said irritated.

"Jeez Grandpa, you need to take a chill pill. I'm sorry, but we need to start getting ready. I need to use your bathroom, please?"

"Ok, I'm sorry Barbie. It's just my hand is starting to hurt again."

"Understand?"

"Yea, okay gramps...or a grumps, I understand."

Michelle couldn't help but chuckle at what Barbie said and Jesse gave Michelle a warning look.

They arrived at Blake Jordans great mansion around 7:00p.m. That evening, Blake made a toast to Michelle and Jesse, on their books being turned into movies, telling them that it was a pleasure being in both of their movies and their upcoming wedding. He also made a toast to Barbie and Stephanie for joining them this evening.

"Oh Blake, ole buddy. Thank you. Thank you a lot. What can we do to repay you for all you have done for us? Not just inviting us all over and great meal, but for being a real true friend, and for being in both of our movies. There isn't too many actors we chose, didn't even consider being in our movies, which was disheartening, but you did. Thank you a million times over."

Blake stuck out his hand, grabbed Jesse's arm, giving it a pat and pulling him in for a brotherly hug.

"It was my pleasure Jesse. In all honesty, we are just regular folks like anyone else. I don't believe in turning down a chance to be in the movies, especially of my fans who want me to be. And the fact that I'm not getting any younger."

As Jesse and Blake continued talking, Michelle slipped away and walked out to the beautiful, huge backyard and watched Barbie, Stephanie and Melody, Blake's girlfriend, in the large pool. Michelle also saw a young gentleman that Barbie was talking to, that she never has seen before. He looked a lot like Blake and she wondered if it wasn't his son. Just then, Blake and Jesse walked out, coming alongside Michelle.

"Son, why don't you put up the net so we can play some water volleyball?"

"Okay dad. Sure will."

"Blake, I was wondering if that was your son. He's the spitting image of you and I think Barb has taken a liking to him."

"Oh yea, he is mine alright. Chip off the old block. He's a good kid and happens to be single at the moment."

After Terry, Blake's son, retrieved the net and hooked it up to the sides of the pool, Michelle, Jesse and him got into the pool.

"Ok, why don't we play a game. The lovely ladies vs. the men? It seems fair. Four beauties and three beasts."

They all laughed and started playing volleyball, with Barbie serving the ball. They played all evening, ending the game with the ladies winning by 3 points. Everyone got out of the pool, with the ladies shivering.

"Ladies, feel free to get in the sauna to get warm and dry off. Us guys will be right here waiting for you around the fire pit with a bottle of chilled wine."

The ladies took him up on his offer and when they had finished, they were welcomed by a chilled glass of sweet red wine as promised. Michelle sat by Jesse, Julianna sat next to Blake, Barbie and Terry sat next to each other, leaving Stephanie sitting in the hanging chair swing. Enjoying one another's company and listening to the mixed genres of music, Terry asked Barbie to dance which she gladly accepted. After the song was over, Jesse took Michelle's hand and asked her to dance. Julianna excused herself to go to the restroom, leaving Stephanie and Blake.

"It looks like we got left behind."

"Apparently", Stephanie chuckled.

"Will you please join me in this dance?"

"I'd be delighted."

He took her hand, leading her to the dance floor where everyone else was dancing.

Chapter Twenty

One week later…

*I*t was the morning of Michelle's and Jesse's wedding as she was woken up by the phone.

"Good morning my Love. How did you sleep, or did you?"

"Mmmmmm, what time is it? I couldn't sleep really. I was too excited about today."

It's 7:07a.m. Excited about today? What's happening today?" he obviously was teasing her.

"Jesse!"

He laughed his wonderful hearty laugh which made her laugh too. Laughter is the best medicine you could ever have, Michelle remembered her Aunt Margaret telling her.

"How did you sleep Jess?"

"Oh I probably got as much sleep as you did, if not less. I was trying to memorize my vows."

"Awe, how sweet Baby. I believe it's much more personal when we just say them to each other rather than repeating them after the preacher, don't you?"

"Yes, but what if I forget them? What then?"

"Then just speak from your heart or we can give them to Pastor Perry for him to prompt us I guess."

"No, If I forget what to say, I will just speak from my heart."

"Awe Jesse, you are going to make me cry."

"Michelle, I want this day to be so perfect for you. I don't want anything to go wrong. We have waited seems like an eternity, for this day to happen. I love you so very much."

"I love you too, beyond measure. You are my extremely Goodlookin, sexy, hunk of a mighty man. This is our day to shine, like sunshine."

"I will be missing you until 12 noon sharp. I can't wait to see my beautiful bride to be."

"Me too Jess, me too. We shall hook up then and finally be Mr. and Mrs. Jesse Lee Fox. YEAH!"

After Michelle hung up the phone, she rolled out of bed, used the restroom, took a shower, shaving her legs last. Her phone began ringing nonstop. It was her mom calling, and then Dawn and Tonia. She told them in no uncertain circumstances not to be late, being at her house no later than 8:45a.m., so they all could be at the beauty shop at 9a.m. Michelle put on what she was going to wear after the wedding and at the reception. She then gathered up all her makeup and jewelry she was going to wear, putting it in a little bag by her wedding dress. The doorbell rang. Michelle saw that it was her mom, her two sisters and niece. They all came in, looking around at the house Michelle and Jesse were buying from the Macafey's.

"Holy Shi...kabobaroonies! I love your house Aunt Monkey!"

Her niece took off, with her two sisters following, touring the house as Michelle looked at the time.

"I'm waiting on Dawn and Tonia to get here. I told them not to be late."

"Calm down Michelle. They will be here."

"I know mom. It's just that we all have to be at Dolly's at 9a.m. sharp. And it's a quarter till."

Her niece and sisters came back into the living room.

"This is a nice place you got here Michelle." Her oldest sister commented.

"Yea it is!" her other sister agreed.

"So how are you doing Aunt Monkey? Are you all packed for your honeymoon?"

"Yea, I believe so."

"Where are we going?"

"Ugh, we aren't going anywhere, but Jesse and I settled on the Alaskan Cruise, I think. We discussed three different places but I told him to surprise me. He certainly is good at doing that."

"Do you have something old, something new, and I know you have something blue since that is one of your favorite colors." her mom asked.

"Yea, I believe so."

Dawn and Tonia came walking up the stairs with Dawn bringing in a beautiful arrangement of flowers, giving them to Michelle.

"Who are these from?"

"Read the card Doofus. We all want to know who they came from like we don't know already."

Pulling out the card, she read it out loud.

"For the love of my life. I love you Michelle, with every beat of my heart, yesterday, today and throughout eternity. My love is forever true. See you soon and DON'T BE LATE ;<}

Always & Forever Yours,

Jesse (Your Sexy, Goodlookin, Mighty Hunky Man)

Michelle didn't read everything he wrote out loud but laughed out loud, shaking her head.

"What else did he say?"

"Oh nothing. We better get going or we are going to be late. Dolly told me in order for all of us to get groomed and styled together, not to be late."

"Yea, we better get to shagging as dad says." her sister said.

"I told Robert and James not to be late or I'd kick their white…a!"

"Okay, Ang, don't say it, but thanks for warning them."

They are filed outside onto the porch as Michelle turned to lock the door.

"What cars we taking? We can take mine, Marcia offered.

"I'll ride with Marcel. Bubbit, you can ride with us."

"Okay mom, you can ride with me, Dawn and Tonia."

"Holy Hillbilly's! Look! It looks like none of us is driving! How cool is that!"

"Okay, which one of you are responsible for this White Limo driving up?"

They all looked at each other, shrugging their shoulders. The limo driver gets out wearing a black top hat, dark sun shades and a black tux, coming around and opens the door for each one to all climb in. Before the limo driver closes the door, Michelle asks the driver who ordered his services.

"Ma'am, I am not liable to say, but to obey my client's wishes. I'm sorry. Is it correct you are going to Dolly's Beauty Parlor, on Heavenly Road?"

"Yes, that is correct. Thank you. One more question. What is your name?"

"Gary, ma'am."

"Thank you Gary."

"The pleasure is all mine, Michelle."

And he closes the door.

"WOW! This is NICE! I bet this cost a pretty penny. Okay, who wants a drink? There are bottles of Pepsi, Diet Pepsi, Dr. Pecker…"

"Angie!" her grandma scolded her as Angela continued to see what was available to drink.

"Red and White wine and Champaign! Wow!"

"Oh Grandma, lighten up. Dr. Pepper, is that better?"

"Yes, much. Thank you."

"Is there glasses? I'll take a glass of campaign, Mary said.

"Yea, they are even chilled, so you can get that frosty mug taste."

They all laughed.

"Hey Angela, I'll take a glass of white wine," Dawn said.

"Diet Dr. Peck, I mean Pepper for me" Tonia said.

Busting out into laughter once again, Edith got onto Tonia like she did her granddaughter.

"Mom, what's your fancy?"

"Oh, I'll try a glass of campaign too."

"Aunt Monkey, what's your fancy?"

"I'm not sure. I'm a bundle of nerves. I'd probably spill whatever I drink."

"Here, I forgot to give this to you earlier. It's a plastic wine glass sippy cup."

Angie pulled it out of her purse as everyone laughed out loud again.

"So, what will it be? Red, White wine or Champagne?"

"Red wine."

After Angela passed out everyone's drinks and poured Michelle her very own wine glass sippy cup with red wine, she poured herself a glass of campaign, holding it up for toast.

"To you and Mr. F., to live long and prosper, enjoying life and each other and May the force be with you. And if Mr. F. ever hurts or upsets you in any way, shape or form, I will personally whip up on him!"

Laughter broke out again, as they toasted and took a drink.

"I don't believe you or I will have to worry about Jesse hurting me in any kind of harmful way babe. Jesse is so good to me and treats me like a princess. Much better than I deserve."

"Okay, that's good. If you ever hurt or upset him, then I'll personally whip up on you Monkey."

After everyone made a toast to Michelle, having very nice things to say, Michelle's mom noticed the dark tinted window that separated them and the driver, was rolled down just a little bit. She could also see someone else sitting in the passenger's seat, but couldn't tell who it was. When she accidentally on purpose put her arm down on the arm rest over some buttons, the window started rolling down more.

"Uh ma'am, please don't touch those buttons. Do you need something?"

He immediately rolled the window all the way up, his voice coming through the speakers.

"Oh I'm sorry."

She still didn't see who was sitting in the front seat because as the window rolled down, the person turned their head immediately towards the other direction.

"Mom, what are you doing? Please control yourself. Michelle said.

"We can't take her anywhere., Marcia teased, laughing.

Her mom was pointing and whispered.

"There is someone else sitting up there. I was trying to find out who it was."

"Really? I thought I heard other laughter besides ours. I wonder who it could be. Surely it isn't Jesse. He knows how important it is to me for him not to see me until our wedding."

"Maybe it's a hitch hiker that needed a ride?"

Everyone laughed again.

"Yea right Dawn. Very funny."

Tonia pushed a button and a voice came through the speaker again.

"Yes?"

"I'm sorry, Is this Gary?"

"Yes ma'am. May I help you?"

"Yes, we were all wondering who was sitting up there with you? It's not the groom to be is it?"

"I'm not liable to say ma'am. I'm sorry. We have just arrived to Dolly's Boutique."

"Okay, thank you."

A few seconds later, the door opened for them as they all got out and walked inside the boutique.

"Well looky here! Y'all made it on time. Dolly said, hugging Michelle's neck.

"Wow, and in style too! That's a pretty nice limo!"

"Dolly, you didn't get the limo for us, did you? Be honest."

"No! I wish I had thought of that. The limo driver is pretty too."

Dolly giggled her adorable giggle as she waved at the limo driver getting into the driver's side. Dolly started on Michelle right away, as her other beauty consultants took care of the other girls.

"Michelle, how do you want me to do your hair? Up? Down? Side?"

"Give her a Mohawk Dolly!" Michelle's mom popped off, laughing.

"Ugh, let's not and say we did." Dolly answered, laughing too.

"I brought a picture how I wanted you to do my hair, but I want your opinion, because I know you wouldn't ever steer me wrong. You are the very best Dolly. I just love you."

"Awe, that's sweet Michelle. What a wonderful compliment and thank you. But you know what they say. Opinions are like, ugh… belly buttons, everyone's got one." and she giggled again. The whole shop roared with laughter.

"That's why I love you so much Dolly. You are so down to earth and just say what you mean. And you sing beautifully too. I'm so glad you agreed to sing at my wedding."

"Awe, it's no problem. Thanks for the roses. You're like family. You are like one of my nieces. I'm honored to do it. But if we don't stop yapping, we won't be on time!"

"Oh, speaking of roses, Jesse had the most prettiest bunch of flowers sent to me, with the nicest card. Dawn must have had orders from him to go pick them up for him because she came walking in with them when they came to the house this morning."

"Oh he did. He does sound like a Prince Charming for all the wonderful things you have told me about him. I just hope he stays this charming, for the rest of your married lives together."

"I can't imagine him any other way. He is my heavenly Darlin. I love him so very much. I have been waiting for him forever and a day or two."

"I know you have. I remember you coming to me that he hurt your feelings or made you mad one reason or another, that you could spit fire at him. Then next time I saw you, you'd be all smiles and giddy that he made your day."

Michelle started laughing and crying.

"Oh Crap! Angela, will you please have Gary take you back to my house and get my wedding dress! I forgot it!"

"Okay Monkey."

Michelle started crying.

"Oh now honey, don't you start that. You will have me crying. It will be okay. Think happy thoughts. Come on now. At least we haven't started your make up yet. You'd look like a guilty raccoon."

Michelle started laughing again.

"There, that's better. Now, be real still and don't mess up your pretty toes or nails. Let's get your hair washed and prettied up now. Where is the picture you was going to show me?"

"Oh, duh. It's in the outside pocket of my purse Dolly. Will you get it please?"

"Sure, is this it?"

"Yea, thanks. What do you think?"

"Awe, that's adorable. This will look great on you, with the contour of your face and all. Yea, this is it. I couldn't have picked one out any better."

Michelle leaned back into the sink, looking up at Dolly.

"Did you have any more ideas for my hair Dolly?"

"No, not really. I figured you wear your hair up. I was thinking of adding some baby's breath and a couple flowers is all."

Dolly finished washing Michelle's hair, trimming it up and then started blow drying it, styling it afterwards. Angela arrived with Michelle's wedding dress.

"Did you find out who is in the front seat Bubbit?", Mary asked, as she was getting her hair washed.

"No, never did, but I had another couple glasses of adult beverage." as she hiccupped.

"She's 21, isn't she Michelle?"

"Oh yea. She's twenty-three."

"Okay, just checking." Dolly said.

By the time Dolly was finished with Michelle, all the other ladies were finished getting their toes, nails and hair done too.

"Thank you so much Dolly, for everything. I don't know how I'm going to repay you for all your generosity and kindness."

"Oh don't worry about it. That's what friends are for girlfriend. I was more than happy to do it. In fact, I'd have been deeply hurt if you didn't let me doll ya'll up. Get it? Doll y'all up?"

Dolly would just giggle her adorable giggle again as everyone else laughed along with her.

"I'm sure you will have a beautiful wedding, but most of all, I pray you'll have a beautiful life together. Jesse is blessed to be getting you. I hope he knows that. But he seems to be a pretty terrific guy who treats you like a queen, as he should and as you deserve."

"Awe, thank you Dolly. Yea, I think he's pretty terrific. In fact, I believe he's responsible for the limo."

"Oh really? He must really love you Michelle."

"He must and worried I'd be late to our wedding so he ordered a limo to hurry me along."

Everyone laughed because they knew how Michelle runs late on occasions.

"Well, I pray God's blessings on you both. I'll see you at the church. Be careful now and don't mess up your hair and nails. I'll bring my little bag full of miracles just in case."

"Again, thank you a million. I can't thank you enough Dolly. You are the greatest!"

Michelle hugged her and they all left as they saw the limo waiting outside. The limo driver was standing by their opened car door as each one slide in. Tonia was carrying her wedding dress, making sure Michelle didn't forget it again.

"Thank you kind sir. Sorry we were a little late."

"That's okay. As long as I get you to church on time, then we have no worries."

The limo drives off to their next destination, which is the church. Angela was looking through the cabinets again.

"Woo, looky here! I thought I looked in all the hiding places. Guess not."

She pulled out a pretty glass bowl full of chocolate covered strawberries and cherries.

"Looks like Mr. F is going to feed you these later on Monkey."

Michelle just laughs as Dawn pours her and Michelle a glass of Champagne, finishing the bottle off.

"I really want to know who was sitting on the passenger's side." Dawn said.

"Me too. Let's ask again. Maybe he will tell us now."

"Ok, you ask this time Tonia."

"Me? I'm curious too but he already told us he couldn't tell."

"Couldn't or wouldn't?"

"Oh I'll ask."

Angela was fumbling trying to find the call button for the speaker and found it.

"Yo limo driver. We really want to know who is sitting up there with you please."

"I'm sorry ladies. That information is highly classified confidential. I am not liable to say or I could lose my job. I have orders from headquarters. I was also told to play this song for the bride to be."

The song, "Chapel of Love" started playing, by the Dixie Cups, and everyone started singing it together. When the song was finished, "Joy to the World" started playing and they all started singing that. By the time they arrived at the church, Angela, Dawn, Mary, Marcia and Michelle were filling the effects of the campaign and wine they had finished off, all singing the last song that was playing by Cyndi Lauper, "Girls Just Want to Have Fun". Michelle saw Pastor Perry walking into the church as they were getting out of the limousine.

"Pastor Perry!" she hollered at him.

"Hi Michelle."

"Thanks Pastor. Her, here are our wedding vows. We decided we'd repeat them after you, because we were afraid of goofing up."

He started laughing.

"Okay, Jesse already gave me his. But you two will do just fine. You have quite a crowd in there Michelle. I'm jealous. If only we could have this big of a crowd on Sunday and Wednesday services."

"Oh Brother Perry, stop it."

He laughed and walked back into the church. Marcia and Mary walked in through the back door, holding the door open for the delivery of the wedding cake. Dawn and Angela went to go see how many people were there already. As they walked back to the room, where Michelle was finishing getting ready, they both caught a glimpse of a guy, standing by a window, in another room. They looked at each other, and at the same time looked into the room again, but he had walked away from the window and out of sight.

"Angela, that wasn't who I think it was, was it?"

Angela started laughing.

"I don't know man, it sure looked like him! Aunt Michelle is going to…!"

Jesse came out of the room just then laughing.

"Oh hi ladies. How's my bride doing?"

"Uh, she's a little nervous Mr. F. How are you?"

"I'm finer than a frog's hair split three ways."

He answered while walking past them into the men's restroom.

They went back into where Michelle was putting on her wedding dress, agreeing before they went in that they not tell anyone who they thought they saw.

"Michelle, you look very beautiful! Very pretty indeed. Jesse will be shell shocked. Get it? Michelle, shell…shocked?"

"Thanks Donna. You are way too funny. Do you hear me laughing? So, how many people are here already?"

"Oh, there are quite a few, on both sides. Even Mr. F.'s side looks as full as ours! I can't believe you are ACTUALLY MARRYING MR. FOX!! Your all time fantasy and dreams coming true. I guess it is true, when they say, time worketh patience."

"Yes my dear niece Angela, it does. It really does."

"I never will forget when you introduced me to him the very 1st time. We rode his bus every morning. I was starting 1st grade, I think, when we had moved by you and grandma and grandpa. We got on the bus and Michelle said, "This is my aunt, I mean my niece." What a goober!"

"Okay Anjoola, will you put my veil on me now, please?"

They all laughed at Michelle.

"What time is it?"

"It's 11:53. We better get ready."

Tony, Michelle's brother in law, started playing the song, the bridesmaids were to walk down the aisle to, which was no other than, "Going to the Chapel." Like no other wedding, Michelle wanted this one to be unique and always remembered. They all lined up together, as each bridesmaid and groomsman walked down the aisle together and stand in their proper spot. Jesse and the pastor would already be standing up front, waiting to see his beloved bride. When it came time for the matron of honor and the best man to walk down the aisle, everyone, including Angel, was astonished! You could have heard a pin drop on the carpet, when they saw who the best man was, except for the exclamation out of Angela's mouth.

"Holy Shhh…kabobs!"

Blake Jordan held out his arm, smiling, to escort Angela down the aisle to stand beside the bridesmaids. Tony started the wedding march and the pastor motioned the congregation to rise and Michelle took hold of her mom and dad's arm to walk her down the aisle. When they started down the aisle, Michelle noticed who was standing next to Jesse. She smiled that much more, looking at them both, they both winked at her smiling as well. No wonder the church was packed out she thought. That's who must have been sitting in the passenger's side of the limo she figured out.

When they were standing in front of Jesse, the pastor motioned them to sit back down.

"Well good afternoon everyone. As everyone knows by now, we are all gathered here today in the presence of God, Angels, families, and friends."

"And freaking good looking Blake Jordan too!" a voice called from the audience, as some laughed and some gasped, realizing it was him. The Pastor continued, after a brief snicker.

145

"To celebrate one of life's greatest moments. To give recognition to the worth and beauty of love, and to add our best wishes and blessing, to the words which will unite Michelle and Jesse in holy matrimony. Who gives this lady to this man?"

In unison her parents say, "We do," as they place Michelle's hand in Jesse's, they go and sit down.

"Marriage is a most honorable union, created and instituted by God, signifying unto us the mystical union, which also exists between Christ and the Church; so too may this marriage be adorned by honesty and true abiding love."

"I'd like to read some scriptures that Michelle wanted me to read. I believe she told me, she had come across these particular scriptures when she was praying for her soulmate to come into her life. But first, I believe Dolly is going to sing the song Michelle has dedicated to Jesse."

When she finished the song, the pastor continued the ceremony.

"These scriptures I am about to read to you, I believe, were how God intended a husband and wife should be united, in perfect harmony. I will be reading out of Genesis 1:27, 2:18, and 1:28."

"So God created man in his own image, in the image of God created he him: male and female created he them. And the Lord God said, it is not good that man should be alone; I will make him a helpmate for him. So God blessed them, and God said unto them, be fruitful, and multiply, and replenish the earth, and subdue it: and have dominion over the fish of the sea, and over the fowl of the air, and over every living thing that moveth upon the earth."

"But a husband and wife should not confuse love of worldly measures for even if worldly success is found, only love will maintain a marriage. Mankind did not create love; love is created by God. The measure of true love is a love both freely given and freely accepted, just as God's love for us is unconditional and free."

"As you travel through life together, I caution you to remember that the true measure of success, the true avenue to joy and peace, is to be found within the two of you, to hold in your hearts for each other, as you do this very moment. I ask you to embrace your love for one another, very tightly, and never let it go. And always keep God in the very core and center of your marriage."

"Within the Bible, nothing is of more importance than love. We are told of the beautiful truth that God is Love. We are assured that, Love conquers all. It is love, which brings you here today, the union of two hearts, two spirits, which will unite and beat as one. As your love and lives continue to interweave as one pattern, remember that it was love that brought you here today. It is love that will make this a glorious union, and it is love that will cause this union to endure."

"Now finally, you two face each other and join hands."

"Jesse Lee Fox, do you take Michelle Renee' Mertz to be your lawful wedded wife?"

"I do."

Wedding rings are an outward and visible sign of an inward spiritual grace and the unbroken circle of love, signifying to all, the union of this woman and this man in marriage."

"Repeat after me. I, Jesse, take you Michelle,"

Tears of joy started streaming down Michelle's face, looking into Jesse's beautiful deep, dark, brown eyes and he repeated his vows. She was so happy, this day had finally came, and that she was marrying her soul mate, and the man of her dreams from long ago.

"And I promise my love to you forevermore."

Jesse continued, without Pastor Garfield's help, bringing Michelle out of her state of bliss.

"With this ring, I thee wed, in the name of the Father, the Son, and the Holy Ghost. Amen and Amen. As the Lord liveth, and thy soul liveth, I will not leave thee. I love you Michelle, my love, yesterday, today, and forever."

Jesse placed the ring on her finger.

"Michelle repeat after me. I Michelle, take you Jesse,"

"I Michelle, take you Jesse,"

Michelle recited it too, without the pastor's help.

"To be my husband, to have and to hold, in sickness and in health, for richer or for poorer, and I promise my love to you forevermore. With this ring, I thee wed, in the name of the Father, the Son, and the Holy Ghost. Amen and Amen. As the Lord liveth, and thy soul liveth, I will not leave thee. I truly love you Jesse, my Darlin, yesterday, today, and forever."

And Michelle slips the ring unto his finger.

The song by George Straitline, I Cross My Heart played, declaring their love to each other, as they mouthed the words of the song to one another.

"A marriage ceremony represents one of life's greatest commitments, but also is a declaration of love. I wish to read you, a couple more scriptures from Ephesians and Corinthians, which I believe is a perfect and true example of love."

"In Ephesians, *the relationship between husband and wife is compared to between Christ and the church: "Submit yourselves unto another as the fear of God. Wives, show reverence for your own husbands, as unto the Lord. For the husband is the head of the wife even as Christ is the head of the church and He is the Savior of the body. Therefore as the church is subject to Christ, so let the wives be to their own husbands in everything."*

"*Husbands, love your wife, even as Christ also loves the church, and gave himself for it; that he might sanctify and cleanse it with the washing of water by the Word; that He might present it to Himself a glorious church, not having spot or wrinkle or any such thing but that it should be holy and without blemish. So ought to love their wives as their own bodies; He that loves his wife loves himself."*

"*For no man ever yet hateth his own flesh; but nourishes and cherishes it, even as the Lord does the church. Fore we are members of His body, of His Flesh, and His bones."*

"And lastly, in Corinthians 13, *Love endures and is kind. Love is not envious or jealous. Love wants not itself. Is not puffed up, does not behave itself unseemingly, seeks not its own, it is not easily provoked, and thinks no evil. Love does not rejoice in unrighteousness, but the truth. Love bears all things, believe all things, hopes all things, and endures all things. Love never fails. So faith, hope, love remains, these three, but the greatest of these is love.*"

"Michelle and Jesse, in so much as the two of you have agreed to love and live together in Holy Matrimony, have promised your love to each other, by these vows, the giving of these rings, and the joining of your hands, I now pronounce you husband and wife. May the Lord bless you and keep you. May He make His face shine upon you, and be gracious unto you. And my He lift up His countenance unto you, giving you perfect peace. Congratulations! Jesse, you may kiss your bride."

"Really? Are you finally finished?" Jesse teased the pastor.

And then Jesse doing just that gave her a long romantic kiss, as everyone was cheering for them. The song, "I Swear", by John Michael played as they walked down the aisle together.

$\mathcal{E}$ pilogue

"I love you Jess, with all my heart, soul, and with every fiber of my being. You are the only one who can turn me on like a radio and make my heart sing nonstop."

"Wow, My Shell. That's quite a compliment. I hope you will always feel like that when I get old and gray."

Michelle started laughing.

"I hadn't heard you call me that in a very long time. And I have always told you, Mr. Fox that age is like very fine wine and cheese. You can only improve as time passes. Age is only a number. And it is up to us to take care of our bodies God has given us, which you have done a pretty good job of. I will see to it that you will continue to and I want you to do the same for me. What do you say?"

"I'm in. Now can we start our honeymoon Love. I want to ravish your beautiful body."

Jesse kissed her passionately, and then started kissing her neck while his warm hand and long slender fingers guided across her bare tummy and soft, smooth tanned legs. He slowly caressed her with his fingertips and she could feel her juices start flowing, just waiting for him. She was like a playground to him, not knowing where to go to next. As his hands cupped her breasts, he kissed one and then the other, sucking and squeezing each one. He then pulled away for a brief moment to slip off her white satin panties as she lay back onto the bed.

Michelle started unbuttoning his shirt and sliding it off, tossing it on the chair that was beside the bed. Her hands roamed over his very well-tanned chest, stopping at one of her favorite places to play, toying, caressing and gently biting his nipple. One and then the other. She called them her pacifiers because they did exactly that. She winked at him before she kissed him passionately and rolled him over onto the bed. At this point, she straddled him, leaning over, kissing his chest again, and running her one hand through his soft brown hair. After she slid off him, her other hand strolled down to the buttons on his trousers, unhook it and pulled them off, revealing his long sexy tanned legs.

Jesse let her have total control as long as he could. Michelle climbed back in bed beside him. She begins roaming her anxious hands slowly over his chest and down to his baby blue boxers, gliding and grazing over his middle section, which was starting to become erect. She lingered there momentarily and then slip her hand inside, caressing him a little more freely and skin on skin. Jesse's soft aggressive moan encouraged her to pull off his boxers and proceeded to continue until he stopped her.

"Michelle Love... I want to make sweet passionate love to you….."

He rolled her back over onto the bed, kissing her with a burning passion, roaming his hands down to her most private place, slipping his fingers inside. Michelle arched up, looking at him with sizzling desire, pleading him to do more. He'd kiss her again, moving his fingers slowly, in and out, making her crave yet more.

"Mmmmmm, Jesse please…"

About the Author

Melody Kay Heart is a new and upcoming number one bestselling author who is sure to win the hearts of millions of readers with her charming wit and inspiration with <u>Time Worketh Patience</u>. Look for her children's book, <u>Lil Moo's Big Adventure</u>. She was born in Wichita, Kansas but has lived most of her 47 years in Oklahoma. In her spare time, she enjoys playing with her three, four legged dog daughters which happen to be 2 Shi-Tzus, Maggie and Melody and Sadie who is a TeaCup Yorkie. She also has faith in God and truly believes if we put our trust in Him in all things, that He will see us through everything. Melody is currently working on more novels to publish and hopes they will turn into movies to inspire her audience of all ages.

<u>*Proverbs 3:5-6*</u>
Trust in the Lord with all your heart, Do not lean on your own understanding, but in all your way acknowledge Him and He will direct your path.

Michelle first saw Mr. Fox when she was in high school, where she developed a serious crush. It's been fifteen years since she graduated from high school, and she's never quite gotten over the way she felt about him. Even as an adult, she always wondered how Mr Fox was doing, talks about finding Mr. Right—or Mr. Heaven as Michelle puts it, and believes Mr. Fox is that guy, the only one for her.

Michelle's best friend, Dawn, has been fixing her up on blind dates to try to get Michelle over her fixation on Mr. Fox. She has tried, time and again, to get Michelle's mind off the handsome history teacher but to no avail. No one compares to him, no matter Dawn's good intentions. Luckily, Michelle has faith that God will make everything work out for the best.

After Michelle graduated, she started writing a novel to help get her mind off the love of her life, and she just finished writing it. Now, she hopes to heal her heart by publishing and sharing her story. Will she accomplish her dream? Will Dawn find Michelle a Mr. Heaven that isn't Mr. Fox? God guides our paths, true, but sometimes, those paths are long and winding.

Melody Kay Heart was born in Wichita, Kansas, but has spent most of her life in Oklahoma. In her spare time, she enjoys playing with her three dogs. She has faith in God and truly believes that if we put our trust in Him, He will see us through everything. This is her first novel. She currently lives in Oklahoma.

Printed in the United States
By Bookmasters